ULTIMATE

THE **CROCKP**

COOKBOOK FOR BEGINNERS

2000 EASY AND DELICIOUS RECIPES
FOR EVERYDAY SLOW COOKING

You don't need to enter any details
except your e-mail

Table of Contents

INTRODUCTION

Crockpot cooking is the best way to save time and energy without sacrificing flavor. A crock pot uses minimal culinary skill, and your patience will result in tender meat and vegetables.

The crock pot is an incredible slow cooker that can cook foods with very little attention over a long period. Crockpot cooking is the perfect way to create inexpensive, home-cooked meals for the whole family.

Some people will say that crock pot food tastes bad or it has a "crock" taste. This will be because they have used seasoning incorrectly or overcooked their food. Seasoning at the beginning of cooking and, as necessary, will fix this problem.

A crock pot is best used on manual, high, or low settings. It is most suited for long slow cooking of meat and vegetables. If you are only cooking once in a while, an electric crock pot may be better suited.

You can use a crockpot for cooking many different kinds of food, such as soups, stews, chili, and much more. A good way to use a crock pot is to put some meat into it and turn it on. If you have time, make some rice or pasta the next day and add the rest of your meal, which will cook while you are relaxing after a long day in school.

Crockpot cooking is very versatile because you can keep your ingredients in the crockpot for a long period without having to worry about spoiling. You can come home from school hungry from eating unhealthy snacks all day so use this technique.

People who do a lot of crock pot cooking will notice that after about 3 days, their crockpot food tastes very similar to the first day. This is because you put your ingredients inside the crockpot, and once the water has boiled, the flavors will blend together.

Crock Pot cooking can be done quickly with easy recipes that do not require a lot of special skills or knowledge. Cooking in a crock pot is not as hard as some people might make it out to be; it just takes some time to get used to it.

In this book, each chapters provides useful information about crockpot and some delicious recipes.

CHAPTER 1

ALL YOU NEED TO KNOW ABOUT CROCK POT

What is Crock-pot?

Crock-pot is a special ceramic pot or stroneware equipped with a heating element. This electrical cooking equipment is used to make meals, particularly when you wish to leave your cooking uncontrolled for hours; however, it cannot be used for boiling, baking, or frying food in oil.

In the 1940s, when women were required to work in locations that were further away from their homes, it was the first time it was used in the United States. At that time, women were required to prepare dinner in the morning before they left for work so that when they returned in the evening, they could successfully complete the food preparation.

The method through which a food is prepared in a crock-pot is known as "slow cooking," thus the name "slow cooker" was coined. Today, a standard slow cooker is constructed of porcelain or glazed ceramic, and it has a circular cover that is typically made of glass. The pot is positioned inside a groove that accumulates condensed vapor and brings about a reduction in the surrounding air pressure.

Thus, a crock-pot, or slow cooker, is a pot made of ceramic that has a heat reservoir. It is used to cook food by allowing it to slowly simmer at a reduced temperature while the user is away from the kitchen.

The slow cooker, often known as a crock-pot, is not the same as a pressure cooker since the pressure cooker works much quicker. Even while both the crock pot and the pressure cooker are functional at atmospheric pressure and produce water vapor while doing so, utilizing a crock pot does not come with any of the risks that are associated with using a pressure cooker.

In other words, a slow cooker is an electric appliance that consists of a ceramic pot that is either round or oval in shape. This pot is topped with a lid that is often made of glass so that the contents within may be seen. Because of the way the device is constructed, it can continue operating even when you are not there. The food in the ceramic pot is heated uniformly by a low electric current, which allows it to cook properly. Even if there are some individuals who are concerned that the electricity in the pot might cause damage to their properties, you should be aware that the electrical unit has a low power that it is perfectly safe to keep it on even while you are not there.

The Major Benefits of a Crock Pot

1. Economical

Due to the obvious low temperature and the prolonged cooking period, you may use cheaper cuts of meat, or you can simply add fewer meat and more vegetables for a meal that is healthy.

2. Much Oil and Fats are not required

When using a slow cooker, there is no need to add any more oil since the food won't cling to the bottom of the pot if it has the appropriate amount of moisture. This reduces the amount of fat that is required for cooking.

When it comes to flavor, fattier does not always equal better in most situations. Since the long, slow cooking period enables flavors to emerge, more oil is not necessary to improve the dish's flavor.

3. You can use the Crockpot without any supervision

You can turn on the crockpot just before leaving for the day, then come back to a cup of hot soup or warm stew without having to worry about whether it is safe to eat or how it will taste. It is OK to keep it on while you are sleeping. What a fantastic way to start the day it would be to have a bowl of warm, hearty oatmeal or any other delicious breakfast dish waiting for you!

4. You don't need any specialized talents in the kitchen

When it comes to slow cooking, all you need to do is add and mix a few ingredients and toss them into the pot. After that, you just need to step back and let the pot work its magic for a few hours.

The flexibility offered by slow cooking is something that can be put to use on a daily basis since it allows you to decide exactly what you want to prepare, when you want to prepare it, with what ingredients, and for how long.

5. It will save you both time and effort.

For once, cooking can stop being a pain and start being something enjoyable since it is so simple to make when you use a slow cooker.

How to Choose a Proper Crock-pot for You?

PROGRAMMABLE OR MANUAL CROCKPOT?

When shopping for a slow cooker, the first thing you need to do is choose whether you want a programmed or manual crock-pot.

Crock-pots that are operated manually often include a knob or button with a few settings that allow the user to turn the device off, adjust the level of heat, and sometimes reheat the food. The manual slow cooker is simple to handle and use, but if the food is not constantly checked, it runs the risk of being overcooked.

With the programmable crock-pot, which has a progressively broad control settings to set the preparation time as you desire. It is more beneficial in the home when you are too busy to be in the kitchen, you are able to set the preparation time as you like.

Programmable crock pots, in contrast to manual crock pots, give room more control over the cooking process, hence minimizing the possibility of overcooking the food.

SIZE

The size of the slow cooker is yet another crucial aspect to take into consideration. Since a crock-pot performs at its peak efficiency when it is at least half full of food, the size of the pot is arguably the aspect that is most important. In addition, the market offers a diverse selection of sizes, so you will want to carefully consider all of your options before making a final choice.

SETTINGS FOR THE TEMPERATURE CONTROL

The temperature control settings of the crock-pot range from the lowest temperature below 200 degrees Fahrenheit to the highest temperature of 300 degrees Fahrenheit, with an average temperature ranging from 165 to 175 degrees Fahrenheit. It is up to you to decide how you would want to change it based on the recipe, how long you plan to cook the dinner, and how much food you will be preparing.

LID

When shopping for a crock-pot, you need to pay close attention to the structure of the cover. If you want to see what you are cooking, it is best to use a lid made of see-through glass rather than one made of plastic or another opaque material. When doing a lot of cooking, having a lid that can be locked is really helpful and is not a terrible idea either.

Crucial Tips for Successful Crock-pot Cooking

CHOOSE THE PROPER MEAT FOR THE DISH.

To get the best result out of your slow cooker, it is crucial to choose the appropriate cut of meat, and you should be aware that steaks, despite their tenderness and juiciness, are among the most challenging cuts. They are so stiff because the muscle contains fibrous connective tissue, also known as collagen. In order to make them juicy, tender, and moist, you need to cook them over a low heat for a long period of time.

ALWAYS CHOOSE THE APPROPRIATE CUT OF MEAT.

When using a slow cooker, the lamb shanks, beef chuck roast, beef short ribs, or pig shoulder is the piece of meat that has to be chosen with the utmost care. Since the meat needs to be cooked for the whole amount of time specified on the package, removing the cover is not an option.

CARAMELIZE THE MEAT BEFORE COOKING

Even if you just drop all the ingredients into the pot at once, you can still get tasty and well-seasoned meat out of the process. Browning the meat before placing it in the slow cooker gives it more flavour and aroma.

Before browning the meat, coat it in flour to thicken the sauce and give it a more solid appearance. The flour will also give the meat a harder appearance. Browning the ground beef is very necessary before using a slow cooker to prepare stew, chili, or meat sauce using ground beef because browning keeps the meat from clumping together and produces an excessive amount of fat.

ENSURE THAT THE CROCK IS NOT OVERFILLED.

Never put too much food in the slow cooker at once. You may not have much time, and if you have a huge number of people to feed, you could be tempted to keep adding a little bit more and a little bit more until the little amount becomes the whole pot.

There are models of slow cookers that have a fill level indicator. An extremely full crockpot will cause leaking and spills, which will make the entire kitchen awkward. If you keep it at half to two-thirds full, you can avoid overfilling. In most cases, the food will be undercooked because certain components of the dish did not get a sufficient amount of steam.

BEFORE COOKING, LET FROZEN INGREDIENTS THAW AND DEFROST

Defrost any significant portions of food that may take a longer amount of time to cook before placing them in the slow cooker. This will ensure everyone's safety, including yours. In most cases, the optimal time to add frozen peas and other frozen vegetables to a dish is between 10 and 20 minutes before the end of the cooking process.

Even though it won't affect the outcome of the meal, never cook a frozen chicken or roast since it is a poor idea and may even cause germs to grow.

ADD DAIRY PRODUCTS LAST

Cheese, milk, and cream are all examples of dairy products, which are emulsified mixtures of water, fat, and protein with varying proportions of water, fat, and protein in each component. When heated over an extended period of time, dairy products disintegrate and split into their individual components, which are then discarded. In addition, if you wish to include any kind of dairy product in your dinner, you should wait until the very end, just before you serve it, to do so.

How to Take Care of the Slow Cooker

Nearly all contemporary slow cookers, including the original Crock Pot, have a stoneware inner pot that is both simple to remove and safe to clean in the dishwasher. On the other hand, if you want to step up your cleaning skill, the methods that are listed below should be able to assist you.

You might try making a combination of baking soda and detergent and sprinkle it over the pot if there is any adhesive residue that has been left behind in the pot. First, let it rest for a bit, and then clean it well to remove any food that has been adhered.

If the approach described above is unsuccessful, the next thing to try is putting roughly a quarter cup of baking soda into the ceramic pot and then filling the rest of the pot with water. After adding a very little amount of soap, let the mixture rest for two to four hours. That should remove any lingering residue.

If you use your pot for an extended period of time, there may be a layer of "crud" that forms at the bottom of the barrel. The most effective method to eliminate this is to fill the pot with water and then add one half cup of distilled vinegar and one and a half cup of baking soda for every three quarts of water. As soon as the ingredients are combined, place the pot on its lowest setting and give it a good washing after every four hours. In the end, you should finish up with a pot that is polished and has a good appearance.

Take a small bowl and pour a little amount of ammonia to it in order to clean the interior walls of the container. Put the bowl into your slow cooker, then cover it with the lid. The next morning, after letting it rest throughout the night, clean the walls! The stains will wipe out quite easily.

CHAPTER 2

APPETIZER RECIPES

Sausage Dip

Time: 6 1/4 hours   **Servings: 8**

Ingredients:
1 can of diced tomatoes
1 pound of fresh pork sausages
2 poblano peppers, chopped
1 cup of cream cheese
1 pound of spicy pork sausages

Directions:
1. Mix all the necessary ingredients in a crock pot.
2. Cook for a total of six hours on a low setting.
3. Serve cool or warm.

Spiced Buffalo Wings

Time: 8 1/4 hours   **Servings: 8**

Ingredients:
4 pounds chicken wings
1 cup BBQ sauce
1 teaspoon hot sauce
1 teaspoon onion powder
1/2 teaspoon cumin powder
1/2 teaspoon cinnamon powder
1 teaspoon salt
1/4 cup butter, melted
1 tablespoon Worcestershire sauce
1 teaspoon dried oregano
1 teaspoon dried basil
1 teaspoon garlic powder

Directions:
1. Put all the ingredients into a slow cooker and mix well.
2. Continue to stir until the wings are completely coated.
3. Cook for a total of eight hours in a low setting.
4. Serve either warm or cool.

Tropical Meatballs

Time: 7 1/2 hours   **Servings: 20**

Ingredients:
2 poblano peppers, chopped   1/4 cup brown sugar
2 tablespoons soy sauce   2 tablespoons cornstarch
1 tablespoon lemon juice   2 pounds ground pork
1 pound ground beef   1 teaspoon dried basil
4 garlic clove, minced   1/4 cup breadcrumbs
1 egg   Salt and pepper
1 can pineapple chunks (keep the juices)

Directions:
1. In a slow cooker, combine the poblano peppers, pineapple, soy sauce, cornstarch, brown sugar, and lemon juice.
2. In a bowl, combine the breadcrumbs, garlic, egg, basil, and ground beef. Mix everything together after adding salt and pepper.
3. Make small meatballs and put them in the sauce.
4. Cover and cook on the lowsetting for seven hours.
5. The meatballs may be served warm.

Glazed Peanuts

Time: 2 1/4 hours   **Servings: 8**

Ingredients:
2 pounds raw, whole peanuts
1/4 cup brown sugar
1/2 teaspoon garlic powder
2 tablespoons salt
1 tablespoon Cajun seasoning
1/2 teaspoon red pepper flakes
1/4 cup coconut oil

Directions:
1. Put all the ingredients in your slow cooker.
2. Cover and cook them on high settings for two hours.
3. Serve warm or cool.

Ham and Swiss Cheese Dip

Time: 4 1/4 hours   Servings: 6

Ingredients:
1 cup of cream cheese
1/2 teaspoon of chili powder
1 can of condensed onion soup
1 pound of ham, diced
2 cups of grated Swiss cheese
1 can of condensed cream of mushroom soup

Directions:
1. Place all the necessary ingredients in a slow cooker.
2. Cook on low settings for 4 hours.
3. Serve the ham and swiss dip warm.

Spanish Chorizo Dip

Time: 6 1/4 hours   Servings: 8

Ingredients:
2 cups grated Cheddar cheese
8 chorizo links, diced
1 chili pepper, chopped
1 cup cream cheese
1 can diced tomatoes
1/4 cup white wine

Directions:
1. Place all the necessary ingredients in your slow cooker.
2. Cook the Spanish Chorizo dip on low settings for 6 hours.
3. Serve the dip cool or warm.

Mexican Dip

Time: 4 1/4 hours   Servings: 10

Ingredients:
2 cups of grated Cheddar cheese
1 can of black beans, drained
2 poblano peppers, chopped
1/2 of teaspoon chili powder
1 can of diced tomatoes
Salt and pepper .
2 pounds of ground beef

Directions:
1. Combine all the necessary ingredients in a slow cooker.
2. If necessary, sprinkle the dish with salt and pepper.
3. Cook for 4 hours on high settings.
4. Serving the dip warm is preferred.

Asian Marinated Mushrooms

Time: 8 1/4 hours   Servings: 8

Ingredients:
1/4 cup rice vinegar
1 cup water
2 pounds mushrooms
1/2 cup brown sugar
1 cup soy sauce
1/2 teaspoon chili powder

Directions:
1. Place all the necessary ingredients in your slow cooker.
2. Cover and cook for 8 hours on low settings.
3. Set aside to cool in the pot before you serve it.

Nacho Sauce

Time: 6 1/4 hours   **Servings: 12**

Ingredients:
4 garlic cloves, minced
2 tablespoons Mexican seasoning
1 teaspoon chili powder
2 pounds ground beef
2 shallots, chopped
1 can sweet corn, drained
2 cups grated Cheddar cheese
1 can diced tomatoes

Directions:
1. Put all the necessary ingredients in the slow cooker.
2. Cook for 6 hours on low settings.
3. It is preferable to serve this dip warm.

Five-Spiced Chicken Wings

Time: 7 1/4 hours   **Servings: 8**

Ingredients:
1/2 cup plum sauce
1/2 cup BBQ sauce
2 tablespoons butter
1 tablespoon five-spice powder
1 teaspoon salt
1/2 teaspoon chili powder
4 pounds chicken wings

Directions:
1. Combine the butter, plum sauce, five-spice, salt, BBQ sauce, and chili powder in a crock pot.
2. Mix well until it is completely coated after adding the chicken wings.
3. Cover and cook the dish for 7 hours on low settings.
4. Serve either warm or cool.

Queso Verde Dip

Time: 4 1/4 hours   **Servings: 12**

Ingredients:
1 pound ground chicken
2 shallots, chopped
2 tablespoons olive oil
2 cups salsa verde
1 cup cream cheese
2 cups grated Cheddar
2 poblano peppers, chopped
1 tablespoon Worcestershire sauce
4 garlic cloves, minced
1/4 cup chopped cilantro
Salt and pepper

Directions:
1. Put all the necessary ingredients in the slow cooker.
2. Add salt and pepper and cook for 4 hours on low settings.
3. It is preferable to serve this dip warm.

Party Mix

Time: 1 3/4 hours   **Servings: 20**

Ingredients:
4 cups cereals
4 cups crunchy cereals
2 cups mixed nuts
1 cup mixed seeds
1/2 cup butter, melted
2 tablespoons Worcestershire sauce
1 teaspoon hot sauce
1 teaspoon salt
1/2 teaspoon cumin powder

Directions:
1. Put all the necessary ingredients in the slow cooker and mix properly until evenly coated.
2. Cook for 1 hour 30 mins on high settings.
3. Serve the mixture warm or cool.

Caramelized Onion Dip

Time: 4 1/2 hours   **Servings: 12**

Ingredients:

4 red onions, sliced   2 tablespoons butter
1 tablespoon canola oil   1 cup beef stock
1 teaspoon dried thyme   1/2 cup white wine
2 garlic cloves, chopped   Salt and pepper
2 cups grated Swiss cheese   1 tablespoon cornstarch

Directions:

1. In a pan, heat the butter and oil. Onions should be added and cooked until they start to caramelize over medium heat.
2. Place the onions and the rest of the ingredients in your slow cooker.
3. Add salt and pepper, then cook for 4 hours on low heat.
4. Serve the warm dip with veggie sticks or your preferred crunchy foods.

Bourbon Glazed Sausages

Time: 4 1/4 hours   **Servings: 10**

Ingredients:

2 tablespoons Bourbon
3 pounds small sausage links
1/4 cup maple syrup
1/2 cup apricot preserves

Directions:

1. Put all the necessary ingredients in the slow cooker.
2. Cover and cook for 4 hours on low settings.
3. Serve the glazed sausages warm or cool, preferably with cocktail sticks.

Sweet Corn Crab Dip

Time: 2 1/4 hours   **Servings: 20**

Ingredients:

1 cup canned sweet corn, drained
1 teaspoon Worcestershire sauce
2 garlic cloves, chopped
1 cup sour cream
1 teaspoon hot sauce
2 tablespoons butter
2 poblano peppers, chopped
1 can crab meat, drained
2 red bell peppers, cored and diced
1 cup grated Cheddar cheese

Directions:

1. Put all the necessary ingredients in the slow cooker and mix.
2. Cover and cook on for 2 hours low settings.
3. Serve the dip warm or cool.

Rosemary Potatoes

Time: 2 1/4 hours   **Servings: 8**

Ingredients:

4 pounds small new potatoes
1 rosemary sprig, chopped
1 shallot, sliced
2 garlic cloves, chopped
1 teaspoon smoked paprika
1 teaspoon salt
1/4 teaspoon ground black pepper
1/4 cup chicken stock

Directions:

1. Put all the necessary ingredients in the slow cooker.
2. Cover and cook for 2 hours on high settings.
3. Serve the potatoes cool or warm.

Blue Cheese Chicken Wings

Time: 7 1/4 hours   **Servings: 8**

Ingredients:
1 cup sour cream
1 thyme sprig
1/2 cup buffalo sauce
2 oz. blue cheese, crumbled
4 pounds chicken wings
1 tablespoon Worcestershire sauce
1 tablespoon tomato paste
2 tablespoons apple cider vinegar
1/2 cup spicy tomato sauce

Directions:
1. Put the tomato sauce, buffalo sauce, Worcestershire sauce, vinegar, blue cheese, sour cream, and thyme in a slow cooker.
2. Add the chicken wings and mix them until completely coated.
3. Cook for 7 hours on low settings.
4. Serve the chicken wings warm.

Creamy Spinach Dip

Time: 2 1/4 hours   **Servings: 30**

Ingredients:
1 can crab meat, drained   2 shallots, chopped
1 cup grated Parmesan   1/2 cup whole milk
1 cup sour cream   1 cup cream cheese
1 tablespoon sherry vinegar   2 garlic cloves, chopped
2 jalapeno peppers, chopped   1 cup grated Cheddar cheese
1 pound fresh spinach, chopped

Directions:
1. Put all the necessary ingredients in the slow cooker.
2. Cover and cook for 2 hours on high settings.
3. Serve the spinach dip warm with vegetable stick or your preferred salty snacks.

Cheesy Bacon Dip

Time: 4 1/4 hours   **Servings: 20**

Ingredients:
10 bacon slices, chopped
Salt and pepper
1/2 cup whole milk
1 cup grated Gruyere
1 teaspoon Dijon mustard
1 cup cream cheese
1 sweet onions, chopped
1 teaspoon Worcestershire sauce

Directions:
1. Put all the necessary ingredients in the slow cooker.
2. Add salt and pepper and cover.
3. Cook for 4 hours on low settings.
4. Serve the dip warm or cool with vegetable sticks, biscuits or other salty snacks.

Artichoke Dip

Time: 6 1/4 hours   **Servings: 20**

Ingredients:
2 oz. blue cheese, crumbled
2 garlic cloves, chopped
2 sweet onions, chopped
1 red chili, chopped
1 cup cream cheese
1 cup heavy cream
2 tablespoons chopped cilantro
1 jar artichoke hearts, drained and chopped

Directions:
1. Add the garlic, heavy cream, chili, artichoke hearts, onions, cream cheese, and blue cheese in a slow cooker and mix.
2. Cook for 6 hours on low settings.
3. When done, add the cilantro and serve warm.

Chili Chicken Wings

Time: 7 1/4 hours   **Servings: 8**

Ingredients:

4 pounds chicken wings   1/4 cup maple syrup
1 teaspoon garlic powder   1 teaspoon chili powder
2 tablespoons balsamic vinegar   1 teaspoon salt
1 tablespoon Dijon mustard   1/2 cup tomato sauce
1 teaspoon Worcestershire sauce

Directions:

1. Mix the chicken wings and the remaining necessary ingredients in a slow cooker.
2. Stir around until completely coated and cook for 7 hours on low settings.
3. Serve the chicken wings warm or cool.

Chipotle BBQ Meatballs

Time: 7 1/2 hours   **Servings: 10**

Ingredients:

3 pounds ground pork
1 bay leaf
2 shallots, chopped
2 chipotle peppers, chopped
Salt and pepper
2 garlic cloves, minced
2 cups BBQ sauce
1/4 cup cranberry sauce

Directions:

1. Add the garlic, ground pork, chipotle peppers, salt, shallots, and pepper in a bowl and mix.
2. Mix the cranberry sauce, BBQ sauce, salt bay leaf, and pepper in your slow cooker.
3. Form small meatballs and place them in the sauce.
4. Cover the pot with its lid and cook on low settings for 7 hours.
5. Serve the meatballs warm or cool with cocktail skewers or toothpicks.

Chipotle BBQ Sausage Bites

Time: 2 1/4 hours   **Servings: 10**

Ingredients:

Salt and pepper
2 chipotle peppers in adobo sauce
1 cup BBQ sauce
1 tablespoon tomato paste
3 pounds small smoked sausages
1/4 cup white wine

Directions:

1. Put all the necessary ingredients in your slow cooker.
2. If necessary, add salt and pepper and cover.
3. Cook for 2 hours on high settings.
4. Serve the BBQ sausage bites warm or cool.

Cheesy Chicken Bites

Time: 6 1/4 hours   **Servings: 10**

Ingredients:

2 roasted red bell peppers
1/4 cup all-purpose flour
Salt and pepper
1 cup cream cheese
1 cup shredded mozzarella
1/4 teaspoon chili powder
4 chicken breasts, cut into bite-size cubes

Directions:

1. Place the bell peppers, cream cheese, salt, chili powder, and pepper in a blender and blend until smooth.
2. Put the mixture in your slow cooker and add the remaining necessary ingredients.
3. Cook for 6 hours on low settings.
4. Serve the chicken bites warm or cool.

Pork Ham Dip

Time: 6 1/4 hours   Servings: 20

Ingredients:

1/2 cup cranberry sauce	2 cups diced ham
1 cup tomato sauce	1/2 cup chili sauce
1 shallot, chopped	2 garlic cloves, chopped
1 pound ground pork	1 teaspoon Dijon mustard
Salt and pepper	

Directions:

1. Heat a pan over medium heat and add the ground pork. While stirring often, cook for 5 minutes.
2. Place the ground pork in a slow cooker and add the remaining necessary ingredients.
3. Add salt and pepper and cook for 6 hours on low settings.
4. Serve the pork ham dip warm or cool.

Honey Glazed Chicken Drumsticks

Time: 7 1/4 hours   Servings: 8

Ingredients:

1 teaspoon rice vinegar
1/2 teaspoon dried Thai basil
1/4 cup soy sauce
2 tablespoons tomato paste
1/4 cup honey
3 pounds chicken drumsticks
1/2 teaspoon sesame oil

Directions:

1. Put all the necessary ingredients in your slow cooker and mix them until they are completely coated.
2. Cover the pot and cook for 7 hours on low settings.
3. Serve the chicken drumsticks warm or cool.

Cranberry Sauce Meatballs

Time: 7 1/2 hours   Servings: 12

Ingredients:

1 egg	3 pounds ground pork
1 thyme sprig	1 pound ground turkey
1 shallot, chopped	1/2 cup breadcrumbs
1 cup BBQ sauce	1/2 teaspoon ground cloves
2 cups cranberry sauce	1 teaspoon hot sauce
Salt and pepper	

Directions:

1. Combine the turkey, ground pork, egg, breadcrumbs, salt, ground cloves, shallot, and pepper and mix well.
2. Combine the BBQ sauce, cranberry sauce, hot sauce, and thyme sprig in your slow cooker.
3. Form small meatballs and place them in the sauce.
4. Cook for 7 hours on low settings.
5. Serve the meatballs warm or cool.

Cheeseburger Dip

Time: 6 1/4 hours   Servings: 20

Ingredients:

2 pounds ground beef	1 tablespoon canola oil
2 sweet onions, chopped	4 garlic cloves, chopped
1/2 cup tomato sauce	1 tablespoon Dijon mustard
2 tablespoons pickle relish	1 cup grated Cheddar
1 cup shredded processed cheese	

Directions:

1. Heat the canola oil in a pan and add the ground beef. Sauté for 5 minutes then add the meat in your slow cooker.
2. Add the remaining necessary ingredients and cover.
3. Cook on for 6 hours on low settings.
4. The dip is preferably served warm.

Bacon Crab Dip

Time: 2 1/4 hours   **Servings: 20**

Ingredients:
1 teaspoon Dijon mustard
1 teaspoon hot sauce
1 cup cream cheese
1/2 cup grated Parmesan cheese
1 pound bacon, diced
1 teaspoon Worcestershire sauce
1 can crab meat, drained and shredded

Directions:
1. Place a pan over medium heat and add the bacon. Sauté for 5 minutes until fat starts draining out.
2. Place the bacon in a slow cooker.
3. Add the remaining ingredients and cook for 2 hours on high settings.
4. Serve the dip cool or warm.

Curried Chicken Wings

Time: 7 1/4 hours   **Servings: 10**

Ingredients:
Salt and pepper
1 cup tomato sauce
1/2 cup coconut milk
4 pounds chicken wings
2 shallots, chopped
1/4 cup red curry paste
1/2 teaspoon dried basil

Directions:
1. Put all the necessary ingredients in a slow cooker and stir properly until completely coated.
2. Add salt and pepper and cook for 7 hours on low settings.
3. Serve the chicken wings cool or warm.

Wild Mushroom Dip

Time: 4 1/4 hours   **Servings: 20**

Ingredients:
1 cup white wine   1 cup cream cheese
1 cup heavy cream   1/2 cup grated Parmesan
1 teaspoon dried tarragon   1/2 teaspoon dried oregano
1/2 teaspoon ground black pepper
Salt and pepper
1-pound wild mushrooms, chopped
1 can condensed cream of mushroom soup

Directions:
1. Put all the necessary ingredients in your slow cooker.
2. Add salt and pepper and cook for 4 hours on low settings.
3. Serve the dip cool or warm.

Mediterranean Dip

Time: 6 1/4 hours   **Servings: 20**

Ingredients:
2 tablespoons canola oil
2 shallots, chopped
2 garlic cloves, chopped
1/4 cup white wine
1 pound ground beef
1/2 cup tomato sauce
4 ripe tomatoes, peeled and diced
1/2 cup black olives, pitted and chopped
1/2 cup Kalamata olives, pitted and chopped
1/2 teaspoon dried oregano
1 teaspoon dried basil
Salt and pepper

Directions:
1. Place a pan over medium heat and add the beef. Cook for 5 minutes then add the shallots and garlic and cook for extra 5 minutes.
2. Transfer the mixture in your slow cooker and add the remaining ingredients.
3. Add salt and pepper and cook for 6 hours on low settings.
4. Serve the dip warm or cool.

Bacon New Potatoes

Time: 3 1/4 hours   **Servings: 6**

Ingredients:
3 pounds new potatoes, washed and halved
12 slices bacon, chopped
2 tablespoons white wine
Salt and pepper
1 rosemary sprig

Directions:
1. Put the wine, potatoes, and rosemary in your slow cooker.
2. Add salt and pepper and top with chopped bacon.
3. Cook for 3 hours on high settings.
4. Serve the potatoes warm.

Bean Queso

Time: 6 1/4 hours   **Servings: 10**

Ingredients:
1 can black beans, drained
1 cup chopped green chiles
1/2 cup red salsa
1 teaspoon dried oregano
1/2 teaspoon cumin powder
1 cup light beer
1 1/2 cups grated Cheddar
Salt and pepper

Directions:
1. Put the oregano, cumin, salsa, beer, beans, chiles, and cheese in your slow cooker.
2. Add salt and pepper and cook on low settings for 6 hours.
3. Serve the bean queso warm.

Pizza Dip

Time: 6 1/4 hours   **Servings: 20**

Ingredients:
1 onion, chopped
2 garlic cloves, minced
1/2 cup grated Parmesan
1/2 teaspoon dried basil
1 pound spicy sausages, sliced
1 red bell pepper, cored and diced
1 yellow bell pepper, cored and sliced
1/2 pound salami, diced
2 cups tomato sauce
1 cup shredded mozzarella
1/2 teaspoon dried oregano

Directions:
1. Place all the necessary ingredients in your slow cooker.
2. Cook for 6 hours on low settings, mixing once during the cooking time to make sure that the ingredients are properly distributed.
3. Serve the pizza dip warm.

Green Vegetable Dip

Time: 2 1/4 hours   **Servings: 12**

Ingredients
10 oz. frozen spinach, thawed and drained
1 jar artichoke hearts, drained
1 cup chopped parsley
1 cup cream cheese
1 cup sour cream
1/2 cup grated Parmesan cheese
1/2 cup feta cheese, crumbled
1/2 teaspoon onion powder
1/4 teaspoon garlic powder

Directions:
1. Put all the necessary ingredients in your slow cooker and mix gently.
2. Cover and cook for 2 hours on high settings.
3. Serve the dip warm or cool with biscuits, crusty bread, or other salty snacks or even vegetable sticks.

Spicy Enchilada Dip

Time: 6 hours 15 mins   **Servings: 8**

Ingredients:
1 pound ground chicken
1/2 teaspoon chili powder
1 shallot, chopped
2 garlic cloves, chopped
1 red bell pepper, cored and diced
2 tomatoes, diced
1 cup tomato sauce
Salt and pepper
1 1/2 cups grated Cheddar cheese

Directions:
1. Put the ground chicken with shallot, chili powder, and garlic in your slow cooker.
2. Add the remaining ingredients and cook for 6 hours on low settings.
3. Serve the dip warm with tortilla chips.

Mixed Olive Dip

Time: 1 hour 45 mins   **Servings: 10**

Ingredients:
1 pound ground chicken
2 tablespoons olive oil
1 green bell pepper, cored and diced
1/2 cup Kalamata olives, pitted and chopped
1/2 cup green olives, chopped
1/2 cup black olives, pitted and chopped
1 cup green salsa
1/2 cup chicken stock
1 cup grated Cheddar cheese
1/2 cup shredded mozzarella

Directions:
1. Put all the necessary ingredients in your slow cooker.
2. Cover and cook for 1 hour 30 mins on high settings.
3. Serve the dip warm.

Spicy Asian Style Mushroom

Time: 2 hours 15 mins   **Servings: 8**

Ingredients:
1/4 cup hoisin sauce
1/4 cup soy sauce
2 garlic cloves, minced
1/2 teaspoon red pepper flakes
2 pounds fresh mushrooms, cleaned

Directions:
1. Combine the soy sauce, garlic, hoisin sauce, and red pepper flakes in a bowl.
2. Put the mushrooms in the slow cooker and drizzle them with the sauce.
3. Cook for 2 hours on high settings.
4. Let the mushroom cool in the pot before serving.

Three Cheese Artichoke Sauce

Time: 4 hours 15 mins   **Servings: 16**

Ingredients:
1 jar artichoke hearts, drained and chopped
1 shallot, chopped
2 cups shredded mozzarella
1 cup grated Parmesan
1 cup grated Swiss cheese
1/2 teaspoon dried thyme
1/4 teaspoon chili powder

Directions:
1. Put all the necessary ingredients in your slow cooker.
2. Cover the pot and cook for 4 hours on low setting.
3. Serve the sauce warm with vegetable sticks or biscuits or even small pretzels.

Mexican Chili Dip

Time: 2 1/4 hours   **Servings: 20**

Ingredients:
1 can black beans, drained
1/2 cup beef stock
Salt and pepper
1 can diced tomatoes
1/2 teaspoon cumin powder
1 can red beans, drained
1/2 teaspoon chili powder
1 1/2 cups grated Cheddar

Directions:
1. Put the tomatoes, cumin powder, beans, chili, and stock in your slow cooker.
2. Add salt and pepper and top with grated cheddar.
3. Cook for 2 hours on high settings.
4. Serve the dip warm.

Boiled Peanuts with Skin On

Time: 7 1/4 hours   **Servings: 8**

Ingredients:
4 cups water
1/2 cup salt
2 pounds uncooked, whole peanuts

Directions:
1. Put all the necessary ingredients in your slow cooker.
2. Cover and cook for 7 hours on low settings.
3. Drain and allow to cool down before serving.

Spicy Glazed Pecans

Time: 3 1/4 hours   **Servings: 10**

Ingredients:
1 teaspoon dried thyme
2 pounds pecans
1/2 teaspoon garlic powder
2 tablespoons honey
1 teaspoon smoked paprika
1 teaspoon dried basil
1/2 cup butter, melted
1 teaspoon chili powder
1/4 teaspoon cayenne pepper

Directions:
1. Put all the ingredients in your slow cooker.
2. Mix well until they are well distributed and the pecans are evenly glazed.
3. Cook for 3 hours on high settings.
4. Allow to cool before serving.

Cheesy Mushroom Dip

Time: 4 1/4 hours   **Servings: 16**

Ingredients:
1/2 teaspoon chili powder
1-pound mushrooms, chopped
1 teaspoon Worcestershire sauce
1 cup grated Swiss cheese
1/4 cup evaporated milk
1 can condensed cream of mushroom soup
1 cup grated Cheddar cheese

Directions:
1. Mix the cream of mushroom soup, evaporated milk, mushrooms, Worcestershire sauce, and chili powder in your slow cooker.
2. Top with grated cheese and cook for 4 hours on low settings.
3. Serve the dip warm or re-heated.

Taco Dip

Time: 6 1/2 hours   **Servings: 20**

Ingredients:
2 pounds ground beef
2 tablespoons canola oil
1 can black beans, drained
1/2 cup beef stock
1 cup tomato sauce
1 tablespoon taco seasoning
2 cups Velveeta cheese, shredded

Directions:
1. Place a pan over medium heat and add the beef. Cook for 10 minutes, stirring often.
2. Put the beef in your slow cooker.
3. Add the remaining ingredients and cook for 6 hours on low settings.
4. Serve the dip warm.

Swiss Cheese Fondue

Time: 4 1/4 hours   **Servings: 10**

Ingredients:
1 garlic cloves
2 cups dry white wine
2 cups grated Swiss cheese
1 cup grated Cheddar
2 tablespoons cornstarch
1 pinch nutmeg

Directions:
1. Rub the interior part of your slow cooker with a garlic clove. Dispose the clove once done.
2. Add all the necessary ingredients and cook for 4 hours on low heat.
3. Serve the fondue warm with croutons, vegetable sticks, or pretzels.

Quick Layered Appetizer

Time: 7 1/2 hours   **Servings: 10**

Ingredients:
4 chicken breasts, cooked and diced
1 teaspoon dried basil
1 teaspoon dried oregano
1 cup cream cheese
1/4 teaspoon chili powder
Salt and pepper
4 tomatoes, sliced
4 large tortillas
2 cups shredded mozzarella

Directions:
1. Mix the chili powder, salt, oregano, cream cheese, chicken, basil, and pepper in a bowl.
2. Begin layering the chicken mixture, tomatoes, tortillas and mozzarella in your slow cooker.
3. Cover and cook for 7 hours on low settings.
4. Let it cool then slice and serve.

Oriental Chicken Bites

Time: 7 1/4 hours   **Servings: 10**

Ingredients:
1 teaspoon smoked paprika
2 tablespoons olive oil
Salt and pepper
1 teaspoon grated ginger
4 garlic cloves, minced
2 sweet onions, sliced
1/2 lemon, juiced
1 teaspoon cumin powder
1 cup chicken stock
4 chicken breasts, cubed
1/2 teaspoon cinnamon powder

Directions:
1. Put all the necessary ingredients in your slow cooker.
2. Add salt and pepper and mix well until the ingredients are completely distributed.
3. Cover and cook for 7 hours on low settings.
4. Serve the chicken bites warm or cool.

Sweet Corn Jalapeno Dip

Time: 2 1/4 hours   **Servings: 10**

Ingredients:
1 pinch nutmeg
2 tablespoons chopped cilantro
4 bacon slices, chopped
1 cup sour cream
1 cup grated Cheddar cheese
1/2 cup cream cheese
3 cans sweet corn, drained
4 jalapenos, seeded and chopped

Directions:
1. Put the corn, jalapenos, sour cream, Cheddar, bacon, cream cheese and nutmeg in a slow cooker.
2. Cook on high settings for 2 hours.
3. When done, stir in the cilantro and serve the dip warm.

Pretzel Party Mix

Time: 2 1/4 hours   **Servings: 10**

Ingredients:
1 teaspoon salt
1 teaspoon garlic powder
1 teaspoon Worcestershire sauce
4 cups pretzels
1 cup crispy rice cereals
1/4 cup butter, melted
1 cup peanuts
1 cup pecans

Directions:
1. Put the pretzels, peanuts, pecans and rice cereals in your slow cooker.
2. Add melted butter and Worcestershire sauce and mix well then add salt and garlic powder.
3. Cover and cook the mixture for 2 hours on high settings. Mix once during cooking.
4. Let it cool before serving.

Maple Syrup Glazed Carrots

Time: 6 1/4 hours   **Servings: 8**

Ingredients:
1 teaspoon salt
4 tablespoons butter, melted
3 tablespoons maple syrup
3 pounds baby carrots
1/8 teaspoon pumpkin pie spices

Directions:
1. Place the baby carrots in your slow cooker and add the remaining ingredients.
2. Mix until the carrots are completely coated.
3. Cover and cook for 6 hours on low settings.
4. Serve the carrots warm or cool.

Balsamico Pulled Pork

Time: 8 1/4 hours   **Servings: 6**

Ingredients:
1/4 cup balsamic vinegar
2 tablespoons soy sauce
1/4 cup hoisin sauce
2 garlic cloves, minced
2 shallots, sliced
1 tablespoon Dijon mustard
2 pounds boneless pork shoulder
2 tablespoons honey
1/4 cup chicken stock

Directions:

1. Put the stock, garlic, shallots, honey, hoisin sauce, vinegar, mustard, and soy sauce in your slow cooker.
2. Add the pork shoulder and stir in the mixture until completely coated.
3. Cover and cook for 8 hours on low settings.
4. Cut the meat into fine pieces and serve warm or cool.

Cheesy Beef Dip

Time: 3 1/4 hours   **Servings: 8**

Ingredients:
2 pounds ground beef
1 pound grated Cheddar
1/2 cup cream cheese
1/2 cup white wine
1 poblano pepper, chopped

Directions:
1. Put all the necessary ingredients in a crock pot.
2. Cook for 3 hours on high settings.
3. Serve the dip preferably warm.

Bacon Black Bean Dip

Time: 6 1/4 hours   **Servings: 6**

Ingredients:
2 shallots, sliced
1 garlic cloves, chopped
2 cans black beans, drained
1/2 cup beef stock
1 tablespoon brown sugar
2 tablespoons Bourbon
Salt and pepper
1 tablespoon molasses
1/2 teaspoon chili powder
1 cup red salsa
6 bacon slices
1 tablespoon apple cider vinegar

Directions:
1. Place a saucepan over medium heat and add the bacon. Cook until crisp then place the bacon and its fat in your slow cooker.
2. Add all other ingredients
3. Cook for 6 hours on low settings.
4. When done, mash the beans partially and serve immediately.

Spicy Monterey Jack Fondue

Time: 4 1/4 hours   **Servings: 6**

Ingredients:
1 pinch salt
1 pinch ground black pepper
2 cups grated Monterey Jack cheese
1 garlic clove
1 cup white wine
1 red chili, seeded and chopped
1 tablespoon cornstarch
1/2 cup grated Parmesan
1/2 cup milk
1 pinch nutmeg

Directions:
1. Rub the interior part of your slow cooker's pot with a garlic clove just to infuse it with aroma.
2. Put the white wine in the pot then add the cornstarch, parmesan, red chili, cheeses, and milk.
3. Add salt, nutmeg, and black pepper and cook for 4 hours on low heat.
4. Serve the fondue warm with bread sticks or vegetables.

Tahini Cheese Dip

Time: 2 1/4 hours   **Servings: 8**

Ingredients:
1 pinch nutmeg
1/4 cup grated Emmentaler cheese
Salt and pepper
1/2 cup tahini paste
1/2 teaspoon cumin powder
1/4 pound grated Gruyere
1 cup whole milk
1/8 teaspoon garlic powder

Directions:
1. Put all the necessary ingredients in your slow cooker.
2. Add salt and pepper if necessary and cover the pot.
3. Cook for 2 hours on high settings.
4. Serve the dip warm.

Tahini Chickpea Dip

Time: 6 1/4 hours   **Servings: 6**

Ingredients:
2 cups dried chickpeas, rinsed
5 cups water
1 bay leaf
Salt and pepper
1 lemon, juiced
1/4 cup tahini paste
2 tablespoons olive oil
1 pinch red pepper flakes

Directions:
1. Put the water, salt, bay leaf, chickpeas, and pepper in a slow cooker.
2. Cook for 6 hours on low settings then drain and transfer in the blender.
3. Add the remaining ingredients and blend until smooth.
4. Serve the dip fresh or store in an airtight container in the fridge.

French Onion Dip

Time: 4 1/4 hours   **Servings: 10**

Ingredients:
4 large onions, chopped
2 tablespoons olive oil
1 tablespoon butter
1 1/2 cups sour cream
1 pinch nutmeg
Salt and pepper

Directions:
1. Put the pepper, salt, olive oil, butter, onions, and nutmeg in a slow cooker.
2. Cover and cook on high settings for 4 hours.
3. When done, let it cool then add the sour cream, salt, and pepper.
4. Serve the dip immediately.

Roasted Bell Peppers Dip

Time: 2 1/4 hours   **Servings: 8**

Ingredients:
4 roasted red bell peppers, drained
2 cans chickpeas, drained
1/2 cup water
1 shallot, chopped
4 garlic cloves, minced
Salt and pepper
2 tablespoons lemon juice
2 tablespoons olive oil

Directions:
1. Put the chickpeas, shallot, water, bell peppers, and garlic in a slow cooker.
2. Add salt and pepper as required and cook for 2 hours on high settings.
3. When done, puree the dip in a food processor. Add the lemon juice and olive oil.
4. Serve or store it in the fridge in an airtight container for up to 2 days.

Pimiento Cheese Dip

b

Ingredients:
1/2 pound grated Cheddar
1/4 pound grated pepper Jack cheese
1/2 cup sour cream
1/2 cup green olives, sliced
2 tablespoons diced pimientos
1 teaspoon hot sauce
1/4 teaspoon garlic powder
1/4 teaspoon onion powder

Directions:
1. Put all the necessary ingredients in a slow cooker.
2. Cover the pot and cook for 2 hours on high settings.
3. Serve the dip warm with vegetable sticks or bread sticks.

Eggplant Caviar

Time: 3 1/4 hours   **Servings: 6**

Ingredients:
2 garlic cloves, minced
Salt and pepper
1 teaspoon dried oregano
1 lemon, juiced
2 large eggplants, peeled and cubed
4 tablespoons olive oil
1 teaspoon dried basil

Directions:
1. Put the olive oil, basil, eggplant cubes, and oregano in a slow cooker.
2. Add salt and pepper and cook for 3 hours on high settings.
3. When done, add the garlic and lemon juice. Mash and mix well with a potato masher.
4. Serve the dip cool.

Sausage and Pepper Appetizer

Time: 6 1/4 hours   **Servings: 8**

Ingredients:
Salt and pepper
4 roasted bell peppers, chopped
1 poblano pepper, chopped
6 fresh pork sausages, skins removed
1 can fire roasted tomatoes
1 cup grated Provolone cheese
2 tablespoons olive oil
1 shallot, chopped

Directions:
1. Add the oil in a frying pan. Add the sausage meat and cook for 5 minutes, stirring often.
2. Transfer the meat in your slow cooker and add the remaining ingredients.
3. Season with salt and pepper and cook on low settings for 6 hours.
4. Serve the dish warm or cool.

Bacon Baked Potatoes

Time: 3 1/4 hours   **Servings: 8**

Ingredients:
1 teaspoon dried rosemary
Salt and pepper
1/4 cup chicken stock
3 pounds new potatoes, halved
8 slices bacon, chopped

Directions:
1. Place a pan over medium heat and add the bacon. Cook until crisp.
2. Put the potatoes in a slow cooker. Add the bacon bits and its fat, and also rosemary, salt and pepper and mix until completely distributed.
3. Add the stock and cook for 3 hours on high heat.
4. Serve the potatoes warm.

Teriyaki Chicken Wings

Time: 6 1/4 hours   **Servings: 6**

Ingredients:
1/2 cup pineapple juice
1/4 cup water
2 tablespoons canola oil
1/2 teaspoon garlic powder
1/2 teaspoon ground ginger
2 tablespoons brown sugar
1 tablespoon molasses
1/2 cup soy sauce
3 pounds chicken wings

Directions:
1. Put all the necessary ingredients in a slow cooker and mix until completely coated.
2. Cover the pot and cook for 6 hours on low settings.
3. Serve the chicken wings warm or cool.

Goat Cheese Stuffed Mushrooms

Time: 4 1/4 hours   **Servings: 6**

Ingredients:
1 egg
1 teaspoon dried oregano
1/2 cup breadcrumbs
12 medium size mushrooms
6 oz. goat cheese
1 poblano pepper, chopped

Directions:
1. Combine the egg, breadcrumbs, goat cheese, pepper and oregano in a bowl.
2. Coat each mushroom with the goat cheese mixture and put them in a slow cooker.
3. Cover and cook the mixture for 4 hours on low settings.
4. Serve the mushrooms warm or cool.

Creamy Potatoes

Time: 6 1/4 hours   **Servings: 6**

Ingredients:
2 green onions, chopped   1 shallot, chopped
4 bacon slices, chopped   2 garlic cloves, chopped
Salt and pepper   2 tablespoons olive oil
1 cup sour cream
1 teaspoon dried oregano
3 pounds small new potatoes, washed
2 tablespoons chopped parsley

Directions:
1. Put the bacon, oregano, potatoes, shallot, olive oil and garlic in a slow cooker.
2. Add salt and pepper and mix until the ingredients are evenly distributed.
3. Cover the pot and cook for 6 hours on low settings.
4. When done, mix the cooked potatoes with sour cream, onions, and parsley and serve immediately.

Pepperoni Pizza Dip

Time: 3 1/4 hours   **Servings: 10**

Ingredients:
1 cup cream cheese
2 red bell peppers, diced
1 cup shredded mozzarella
2 shallots, chopped
1/2 teaspoon dried basil
1/2 cup black olives
1 1/2 cups pizza sauce
4 peperoni, sliced

Directions:
1. Mix the pizza sauce and the remaining ingredients in your slow cooker.
2. Cover the pot and cook for 3 hours on low settings.
3. Serve the dip warm with bread sticks or tortilla chips.

Beer Cheese Fondue

Time: 2 1/4 hours   **Servings: 8**

Ingredients:
1 shallot, chopped   1 garlic clove, minced
1 cup grated Gruyere cheese 2 cups grated Cheddar
1 tablespoon cornstarch   1 cup beer
1 teaspoon Dijon mustard   Salt and pepper
1/2 teaspoon cumin seeds

Directions:
1. Put the cumin seeds, cheese, cheddar, cornstarch, shallot, garlic, mustard, and beer in your slow cooker.
2. Add salt and pepper and mix well.
3. Cover the pot and cook for 2 hours on high settings.
4. Serve the fondue warm.

CHAPTER 3
CHICKEN RECIPES

Orange Glazed Chicken

Time: 6 hrs. 15 minutes.   **Servings: 6**

Ingredients:
1 cup vegetable stock	Salt and pepper.
1 orange, zested and juiced	6 chicken thighs
1/4 tsp. cumin powder	2 tbsp. olive oil
1 tbsp. balsamic vinegar	1 tbsp. cornstarch
2 sweet onions, sliced.	
1/2 tsp. Worcestershire sauce	

Directions:
1. Put the chicken, orange zest, orange juice, olive oil, onions, stock, cornstarch, balsamic vinegar, Worcestershire sauce and cumin powder in your crock pot.
2. Add salt and pepper and cook the chicken for 6 hours on low settings.
3. Serve the chicken warm.

Chicken Barley Squash Salad

Time: 6 hrs. 15 minutes.   **Servings: 8**

Ingredients:
1-lb. ground chicken	2 garlic cloves, chopped.
1 cup pearl barley	1 cup green peas
2 cups vegetable stock	1 sweet onion, chopped.
2 tbsp. chopped parsley	2 tbsp. olive oil
Salt and pepper to taste.	Lemon juice for serving
2 cups butternut squash cubes	

Directions:
1. Place a saucepan over medium heat and add the bacon. chicken. Cook for a few minutes then place in your crock pot.
2. Add the remaining ingredients, and also salt and pepper.
3. Cook for 6 hours on low settings.
4. Serve the Salad warm and fresh, sprinkled with lemon juice.

BBQ Chicken

Time: 8 hrs. 15 minutes.   **Servings: 8**

Ingredients:
1/2 tsp. chili powder	1 tsp. Worcestershire sauce
2 tbsp. lemon juice	2 tbsp. maple syrup
1 cup BBQ sauce	1/2 cup vegetable stock
1 tsp. mustard seeds	1/2 tsp. garlic powder
Salt and pepper	
4 chicken breasts, boneless and skinless, halved	

Directions:
1. Put all the necessary ingredients in your crock pot.
2. Add salt and pepper and cook for 8 hours on low settings.
3. Serve the chicken warm with your favorite additional dish.

Multigrain Chicken Pilaf

Time: 6 hrs. 30 minutes.   **Servings: 8**

Ingredients:
2 cups vegetable stock	1 cup frozen edamame
1 cup green peas	1/2 cup wild rice
1/2 cup pearl barley	1 leek, sliced.
2 garlic cloves, chopped.	Salt and pepper
1/2 tsp. dried sage	1/2 tsp. dried oregano
2 chicken breasts, cubed.	
1 sweet potato, peeled and cubed.	
1 tbsp. chopped parsley for serving	

Directions:
1. Put the stock, sage, chicken, leek, garlic, edamame, green peas, sweet potatoes, wild rice, pearl barley, and oregano in your crock pot.
2. Add salt and pepper and cook for 6 hours on low settings.
3. When done, add the parsley and serve warm.

Cream Cheese Chicken

Time: 4 hrs. 15 minutes.   Servings: 4
Ingredients:
1/2 cup chicken stock
1 sweet onion, chopped.
4 chicken breasts
1-can cream of chicken soup
1 tsp. dried Italian herbs
1 cup cream cheese
4 garlic cloves, minced.
2 tbsp. butter Salt and pepper

Directions:
1. Add salt, pepper, and Italian herbs to the Chicken. Dissolve the butter in a saucepan and add the chicken. Cook and then place the chicken in your crock pot.
2. Add the remaining ingredients and adjust the taste with salt and pepper.
3. Cook on low settings for 4 hours. Serve the chicken warm.

Chicken Sweet Potato Stew

Time: 3 hrs. 15 minutes.   Servings: 6
Ingredients:
2 tbsp. butter
2 shallots, chopped.
1 pinch cinnamon powder
1½ cups vegetable stock
1/2 tsp. cumin powder
2 chicken breasts, cubed.
2-lbs. sweet potatoes, peeled and cubed.
1/2 tsp. garlic powder
Salt and pepper.

Directions:
1. Put the butter, chicken, and shallots in your crock pot. Cook for 5 minutes then place in your crock pot.
2. Add the sweet potatoes, cumin powder, garlic and cinnamon, as well as stock, salt and pepper.
3. Cook for 3 hours on high settings. Serve the stew warm or cool.

Adobo Chicken with Bok Choy

Time: 6 hrs. 30 minutes.   Servings: 4
Ingredients:
4 chicken breasts
1 cup chicken stock
4 garlic cloves, minced.
1 sweet onion, chopped.
1 head bok choy, shredded
2 tbsp. soy sauce
1 tbsp. brown sugar
1 tsp. paprika

Directions:
1. Put the paprika, onion, soy sauce, chicken, garlic, brown sugar, and stock in your crock pot.
2. Cook for 4 hours on low settings then add the bok choy. Continue cooking for extra 2 hours.
3. Serve the chicken and bok choy warm.

Chicken Taco Filling.

Time: 6 hrs. 15 minutes.   Servings: 8
Ingredients:
1/2 tsp. celery seeds
1/2 tsp. cumin powder
1 tbsp. taco seasoning
1/4 tsp. chili powder
4 chicken breasts, halved
1 cup chicken stock

Directions:
1. Put all the necessary ingredients in your crock pot. Add salt and pepper.
2. Cook for 6 hours on low settings.
3. When done, shred the meat into fine threads and serve it in taco shells.

Paprika Chicken Wings.

Time: 3 hrs. 15 minutes.   Servings: 4
Ingredients:
Salt and pepper
2-lbs. chicken wings
1½ tsp. smoked paprika
1 tbsp. honey
1/2 tsp. sweet paprika
1/2 cup chicken stock.

Directions:
1. Put the honey, salt, chicken wings, paprika, and pepper in your crock pot.
2. Add the stock then cover and cook for 3 hours on high settings.
3. Serve the chicken warm and fresh with your favorite side dish.

Red Wine Chicken and Mushroom Stew

Time: 6 hrs. 30 minutes.   Servings: 6
Ingredients:
1 large onion, chopped.
4 garlic cloves, minced.
1 bay leaf
1 thyme sprig
Salt and pepper
6 chicken thighs
4 cups sliced mushrooms
1/2 cup red wine
1 cup chicken stock.

Directions:
1. Put the stock, bay leaf, onion, garlic, mushrooms, chicken, red wine, and thyme in your crock pot.
2. Add salt and pepper and cook for 6 hours on low settings.
3. Serve the stew warm and fresh.

Curry Braised Chicken.

Time: 8 hrs. 15 minutes.   Servings: 6
Ingredients:
1/2 tsp. cumin powder   1/4 tsp. chili powder
1 tsp. curry powder   1/2 tsp. onion powder
Salt and pepper   1 tsp. garlic powder
1 cup chicken stock   1 tbsp. grated ginger
6 chicken thighs   1/2 cup plain yogurt
Cooked white rice for serving

Directions:
1. Combine the chicken with onion, curry powder, garlic powder, cumin, ginger, and chili powder.
2. Transfer the chicken to the crock pot then add the yogurt and stock.
3. Add salt and pepper and cook for 8 hours on low settings.
4. Serve the chicken warm with cooked white rice.

Chicken Layered Potato Casserole

Time: 6 hrs. 30 minutes.   Servings: 8
Ingredients:
2-lbs. potatoes, peeled and sliced.
1 cup heavy cream
1½ cups whole milk
2 chicken breasts, cut into thin strips
1/4 tsp. chili powder
1/4 tsp. onion powder
1/4 tsp. cumin powder
1/2 tsp. garlic powder
Salt and pepper to taste.

Directions:
1. Put the cumin powder, garlic powder, cream, milk, chili powder, and onion powder.
2. Place the potatoes and chicken in your slow cooker.
3. Pour the milk mixture over the potatoes and chicken then add salt and pepper.
4. Cook for 6 hours on low settings. Serve the casserole warm or cool.

Greek Orzo Chicken

Time: 6 hrs. 30 minutes.   Servings: 6
Ingredients:
Salt and pepper
2 chicken breasts, cubed.
1 celery stalk, diced
1/2 tsp. dried basil
1 tsp. dried oregano
2 ripe tomatoes, peeled and diced.
1/4 cup pitted Kalamata olives
2 cups chicken stock
1/2 tsp. dried parsley
1 cup orzo, rinsed.
Feta cheese for serving.

Directions:
1. Place the orzo and the remaining ingredients in the crock pot.
2. Add salt and pepper and cook for 6 hours on low settings.
3. Serve the chicken warm and top with feta cheese.

Spiced Butter Chicken

Time: 6 hrs. 45 minutes.   Servings: 6
Ingredients:
6 chicken thighs   1 large onion, chopped.
4 garlic cloves, chopped. 1½ cups coconut milk
2 tbsp. butter   1 tsp. curry powder
1 tsp. garam masala   1/2 tsp. cumin powder
1/4 tsp. chili powder   Salt and pepper.
1/2 cup plain yogurt for serving

Directions:
1. Heat the butter in the slow cooker. Add the chicken and cook until it turns golden brown.
2. Place the chicken in your slow cooker and add the remaining ingredients.
3. Cook for 6 hours on low settings.
4. Serve the chicken warm.

Garden Chicken Stew

Time: 8 hrs. 30 minutes.   Servings: 8
Ingredients:
1 onion, chopped.
1 tsp. dried oregano
1 cup tomato sauce
2 cups chicken stock
4 large potatoes, peeled and cubed.
2 carrots, sliced.
1/2 tsp. dried basil
3 chicken breasts, cubed.
1-can (15 oz. white beans, drained.
2 tbsp. canola oil
2 celery stalks, sliced.
2 ripe tomatoes, peeled and diced.
Salt and pepper.

Directions:
1. Put all the necessary ingredients in your crock pot.
2. Add salt and pepper and cook the stew for 8 hours on low settings until the chicken and veggies are tender.
3. Serve the stew warm.

Spiced Chicken over Wild Rice

Time: 7 hrs. 15 minutes.   Servings: 6
Ingredients:
2 cups sliced mushrooms
2 celery stalk, diced
6 chicken thighs
1 carrot, diced
1/2 tsp. chili powder
Salt and pepper
2 cups vegetable stock
1 cup wild rice
1 tsp. cumin powder.
Directions:
1. Sprinkle the chicken with salt, cumin powder, chili, and pepper.
2. Put the carrot, mushrooms, stock, rice, and celery in your crock pot.
3. Put the chicken on top and cook for 7 hours on low settings.
4. Serve the chicken and rice warm or chilled.

Turmeric Chicken Stew

Time: 6 hrs. 30 minutes.   Servings: 6
Ingredients:

1 cup tomato sauce
1 cup chicken stock
2 tbsp. canola oil
2 chicken breasts, cubed
15 oz. chickpeas, drained.
2 red bell peppers, cored and diced.
2 cups fresh spinach, shredded
1/2 head cauliflower, cut into florets
1 cup coconut milk
Salt and pepper
1 tsp. turmeric powder 1-can

Directions:

1. Season the chicken with salt, pepper, and turmeric powder.
2. Heat the canola oil in a pan and add the chicken. Cook for a few minutes until golden.
3. Place the chicken in your slow cooker then add the remaining ingredients.
4. Sprinkle with salt and pepper and cook for 6 hours on low settings. Serve the dish warm.

Honey Garlic Chicken Thighs with Snap Peas

Time: 6 hrs. 15 minutes.   Servings: 6
Ingredients:

6 chicken thighs
1/4 cup vegetable stock
3 tbsp. honey
1/2 tsp. smoked paprika
1-lb. snap peas
2 tbsp. soy sauce
1/2 tsp. cumin powder
1/2 tsp. fennel seeds

Directions:

1. Put the cumin powder, paprika, chicken, honey, fennel seeds, and soy sauce in a bowl and mix well.
2. Combine the snap peas and stock in your crock pot.
3. Place the chicken over the snap peas and cover.
4. Cook for 6 hours on low settings.
5. Serve the chicken and snap peas warm.

Vegetable Braised Chicken

Time: 7 hrs. 30 minutes.   Servings: 8
Ingredients:

1 rosemary sprig
2 cups vegetable stock
Salt and pepper
2 carrots, sliced
2 celery stalks, sliced
1 parsnip, sliced
4 chicken breasts, cut into smaller pieces
1 thyme sprig
2 large potatoes, peeled and cubed.

Directions:

1. Put all the necessary ingredients in your slow cooker. Add salt and pepper and cover.
2. Cook for 7 hours on low settings.
3. Serve the chicken warm.

Parmesan Chicken.

Time: 6 hrs. 15 minutes.   Servings: 4
Ingredients:

1½ cups grated Parmesan
1/2 tsp. cumin powder
4 chicken breasts
1/2 cup chicken stock
1/4 tsp. chili powder
1 tsp. dried thyme
Salt and pepper.

Directions:

1. Put the chicken with salt, cumin powder, chili powder, parmesan, pepper, and thyme in the crock pot.
2. Add the stock in the pot and top the chicken with grated cheese.
3. Cook for 6 hours on low settings.
4. Serve the chicken warm.

Cider Braised Chicken

Time: 8 hrs. 15 minutes.   Servings: 8
Ingredients:
1 tsp. cumin powder
Salt and pepper
1½ cups apple cider
1 tsp. dried thyme
1 whole chicken, cut into smaller pieces
1 tsp. dried oregano.

Directions:
1. Sprinkle the chicken with oregano, pepper, salt, thyme, and cumin powder and put it in your crock pot.
2. Add the apple cider and cook for 8 hours on low settings.
3. Serve the chicken warm with your favorite dish.

Soy Braised Chicken

Time: 3 hrs. 15 minutes.   Servings: 6
Ingredients:
 1/4 cup apple cider
2 shallots, sliced.
1 bay leaf
1/2 tsp. cayenne pepper
Salt and pepper to taste
1/4 cup soy sauce
6 chicken thighs
2 garlic cloves, chopped
1 tbsp. brown sugar
Cooked white rice for serving.

Directions:
1. Put the chicken, apple cider, soy sauce, shallots, garlic cloves, bay leaf, brown sugar, and cayenne pepper in the crock pot.
2. Add salt and pepper if necessary and cook for 3 hours on high settings.
3. Serve the chicken warm.

Chicken Black Olive Stew

Time: 6 hrs. 15 minutes.   Servings: 6
Ingredients:
1/4 tsp. chili powder
6 chicken thighs
1/2 cup tomato sauce
1/4 cup dry white wine
2 tbsp. tomato paste
1/2 cup pitted black olives
1/2 cup pitted Kalamata olives
1 shallot, chopped.
1-can (28 oz. diced tomatoes
2 tbsp. olive oil
4 garlic cloves, minced.
Salt and pepper.

Directions:
1. Put all the necessary ingredients in your crock pot, adding salt and pepper to taste.
2. Cook for 6 hours on low settings.
3. Serve the stew warm.

Fennel Braised Chicken

Time: 6 hrs. 15 minutes.   Servings: 4
Ingredients:
2 oranges, juiced
1 bay leaf
4 chicken breasts
2 carrots, sliced.
1 sweet onion, sliced.
Salt and pepper.
1½ cups chicken stock
1 fennel bulb, sliced.

Directions:
1. Put all the necessary ingredients in your crock pot.
2. Add salt and pepper and cook for 6 hours on low settings.
3. Serve the chicken warm.

Korean BBQ Chicken

Time: 3 hrs. 15 minutes.   Servings: 4
Ingredients:
1/2 cup chicken stock
1 green onion, chopped.
1 tsp. chili paste
4 boneless and skinless chicken breasts
2 tbsp. brown sugar
1 tbsp. rice vinegar
6 garlic cloves, minced.
1/4 cup soy sauce
1 tsp. grated ginger

Directions:
1. Combine the chicken and the remaining ingredients in the crock pot.
2. Cover and cook for 3 hours on high settings.
3. Serve the chicken warm.

White Chicken Cassoulet

Time: 6 hrs. 15 minutes.   Servings: 8
Ingredients:
2 carrots, sliced.
1 cup chicken stock
1 large onion, chopped.
2 garlic cloves, chopped.
1/4 cup dry white wine
2 celery stalks, sliced.
2 tbsp. canola oil
Salt and pepper
4 chicken breasts, cubed.
2 cans (15 oz. each white beans).

Directions:
1. Heat the oil in a clean pan and add the chicken.
2. Fry for a few minutes until golden then place the chicken in the slow cooker.
3. Add the remaining ingredients in your crock pot and add salt and pepper.
4. Cook for 6 hours on low settings.
5. Serve the cassoulet warm.

Medley Vegetable Chicken Stew

Time: 8 hrs. 15 minutes.   Servings: 8
Ingredients:
2 sweet potatoes, peeled and cubed.
1-can (15 oz. chickpeas, drained.
1 cup vegetable stock
1/2 tsp. chili powder
1/2 tsp. dried oregano
Salt and pepper
2 carrots, sliced.
1-can fire roasted tomatoes
8 chicken drumsticks
1 onion, chopped.
4 garlic cloves, chopped.
1 celery stalk, sliced.
1/2 tsp. cumin powder

Directions:
1. Put the chicken, vegetables, spices, and stock in the crock pot.
2. Sprinkle with salt and pepper and cook for 8 hours on low settings.
3. Serve the stew warm and fresh.

Chicken Cauliflower Gratin

Time: 6 hrs. 15 minutes.   Servings: 6
Ingredients:
1½ cups grated Cheddar Cheese
2 chicken breasts, cubed.
1 pinch cayenne pepper
Salt and pepper
1/2 tsp. garlic powder
1 head cauliflower, cut into florets
1-can condensed cream of chicken soup

Directions:
1. Put the chicken soup, salt, garlic powder, cayenne pepper, cauliflower, chicken, and pepper in your crock pot.
2. Top with grated cheese and cook for 6 hours on low settings.
3. Serve the dish warm.

Chicken Tikka Masala

Time: 2 hrs. 30 minutes.   Servings: 4
Ingredients:
4 chicken thighs
1 cup coconut milk 1 cup diced tomatoes
1 lime, juiced
2 tbsp. tomato paste
Chopped cilantro for serving
1/2 cup chicken stock
2 shallots, chopped.
4 garlic cloves, minced.
Cooked rice for serving
1 tbsp. garam masala
2 tbsp. canola oil
Salt and pepper.

Directions:
1. Heat the oil in a clean pan and add the chicken. Cook until golden then place the chicken in your slow cooker.
2. Add the remaining ingredients and sprinkle with salt and pepper.
3. Cook for 2 hours on high settings.
4. Serve the dish warm, topped with chopped cilantro, over cooked rice.

Sesame Glazed Chicken

Time: 3 hrs. 15 minutes.   Servings: 6
Ingredients:
2 tbsp. fresh orange juice
2 tbsp. hoisin sauce
1 tsp. grated ginger
2 tbsp. water
1 tbsp. sesame seeds
6 chicken thighs
1 tbsp. cornstarch
1 tbsp. sesame oil
2 tbsp. soy sauce
1 tbsp. brown sugar

Directions:
1. Put all the necessary ingredients in your crock pot.
2. Cook the chicken for 3 hours on high settings.
3. Serve the chicken warm with your favorite

Cheesy Chicken.

Time: 2 hrs. 15 minutes.   Servings: 2
Ingredients:
1 cup cream of chicken soup
1/4 tsp. garlic powder
2 chicken breasts
1 cup grated Cheddar
Salt and pepper.

Directions:
1. Put all the remaining ingredients in the crock pot.
2. Add salt and pepper and cover.
3. Cook for 2 hours on high settings.
4. Serve the chicken warm, topped with plenty of cheesy sauce.

Tomato Soy Glazed Chicken.

Time: 8 hrs. 15 minutes.   Servings: 8
Ingredients:
1/2 cup tomato sauce
2 tbsp. brown sugar
8 chicken thighs
1/2 cup soy sauce
1 tsp. chili powder

Directions:
1. Put all the necessary ingredients in your crock pot.
2. Cook the chicken for 8 hours on low settings.
3. Serve the chicken warm.

Chicken Stroganoff

Time: 6 hrs. 15 minutes.   Servings: 6
Ingredients:
2 shallots, chopped.
2 cups sliced mushrooms
1 cup vegetable stock
1 tsp. dried Italian herbs
Salt and pepper
2 tbsp. butter
2 garlic cloves, chopped.
3 chicken breasts, cubed.
1 cup cream cheese
2 celery stalks, sliced.
Cooked pasta of your choice for serving.

Directions:
1. Heat the butter in a pan and add the chicken. Cook until golden then place in the crock pot.
2. Add the remaining ingredients and sprinkle with salt and pepper.
3. Cook for 6 hours on low settings.
4. Serve Warm

Creamy Chicken Stew

Time: 6 hrs. 15 minutes.   Servings: 6
Ingredients:
2 potatoes, peeled and cubed.
1 cup vegetable stock
1 shallot, sliced.
2 tbsp. olive oil
Salt and pepper
1-can condensed cream of chicken soup
3 chicken breasts, cubed.
1/2 head cauliflower, cut into florets
1 celery stalk, sliced.

Directions:
1. Heat the oil in a clean frying pan and add the chicken. Cook for a few minutes until it turns gold.
2. Transfer the chicken in your crock pot.
3. Add the remaining ingredients and sprinkle with salt and pepper.
4. Cook the stew for 6 hours on low settings.
5. Serve the stew warm.

Pulled Chicken

Time: 8 hrs. 15 minutes.   Servings: 8
Ingredients:
1 tsp. grated ginger
1 cup BBQ sauce
2 large sweet onions, sliced.
4 chicken breasts
1 cup apple cider
Salt and pepper.

Directions:
1. Put all the necessary ingredients in your crock pot. Add salt and pepper as needed.
2. Cook for 8 hours on low settings.
3. When done, shred the chicken into fine threads using two forks.
4. Serve the chicken warm.

Sweet Glazed Chicken Drumsticks

Time: 5 hrs. 15 minutes.   Servings: 4
Ingredients:
2-lbs. chicken drumsticks
2 green onions, chopped.
1 cup pineapple juice
1/4 cup chicken stock
2 tbsp. soy sauce
2 tbsp. brown sugar
1 tsp. grated ginger
1/4 tsp. chili powder
White rice for serving
Salt and pepper
Directions:

1. Put the brown sugar, chili, pineapple juice, soy sauce, drumsticks, ginger, stock, and green onions in the crock pot.
2. Add salt and pepper and cook for 5 hours on low settings.
3. Serve the dish warm, over cooked white rice.

Thai Chicken Vegetable Medley

Time: 4 hrs. 15 minutes.   Servings: 6
Ingredients:
2 cups button mushrooms
4 garlic cloves, minced.
1 leek, sliced.
1 tbsp. red Thai curry paste
Salt and pepper
1/2 cup vegetable stock
2 zucchinis, sliced.
2 red bell peppers, cored and sliced
2 chicken breasts, cut into strips
2 heirloom tomatoes, peeled and diced.
1 cup coconut milk.

Directions:
1. Put all the necessary ingredients in your crock pot. Add salt and pepper and cover.
2. Cook for 4 hours on low settings.
3. Serve the dish warm or cool.

Cordon Bleu Chicken

Time: 6 hrs. 15 minutes.   Servings: 4
Ingredients:
4 chicken breasts, boneless and skinless
4 thick slices ham
4 slices Cheddar cheese
1/2 cup vegetable stock
Salt and pepper.
1 tsp. dried thyme

Directions:
1. Add salt, pepper, and thyme to the chicken and place it in your crock pot.
2. Add a slice of ham and cheese and pour the stock in.
3. Cook for 6 hours on low settings.
4. Serve the chicken warm.

Hoisin Chicken

Time: 2 hrs. 30 minutes.   Servings: 6
Ingredients:
3 chicken breasts, sliced.   2 carrots, sliced.
1 tsp. sesame oil   2 tbsp. sesame seeds
1 tbsp. soy sauce   1/4 cup chicken stock
1/4 cup hoisin sauce
2 garlic cloves, minced.
2 green onions, chopped.

Directions:
1. Put the hoisin sauce, soy sauce, carrots, chicken stock, chicken, sesame oil, sesame seeds, and garlic in your crock pot.
2. Cover and cook for 2 hours 25minutes on high settings.
3. Serve the chicken warm, topped with green onions.

Mango Chicken Sauté.

Time: 2 hrs. 45 minutes.   Servings: 6
Ingredients:
1-can fire roasted tomatoes
1/4 tsp. grated ginger
Salt and pepper.
1 cup chicken stock
1 chipotle pepper, chopped.
4 garlic cloves, chopped.
2 tbsp. canola oil
1/2 tsp. cumin powder
1 large sweet onion, sliced.
2 chicken breasts, cut into thin strips
1 large mango, peeled and cubed.

Directions:
1. Heat the canola oil in your crock pot and add the chicken. Cook for a few minutes until golden brown.
2. Place the chicken in your crock pot. Add the remaining ingredients and cover the pot.
3. Cook the chicken sauté for 2½ hours on high settings. Serve the dish warm.

Spicy Hot Chicken Thighs.

Time: 8 hrs. 15 minutes.   Servings: 8
Ingredients:
1/2 tsp. garlic powder
1/2 tsp. cumin powder
Salt and pepper
1/2 cup vegetable stock
1/4 cup hot sauce
8 chicken thighs
1/2 cup tomato sauce
2 tbsp. butter.

Directions:
1. Mix the chicken thighs with the remaining ingredients, including salt and pepper in the crock pot.
2. Cover and cook the mixture for 8 hours on low settings.
3. Serve the chicken thighs warm.

Chicken Ravioli In Tomato Sauce.

Time: 2 hrs. 45 minutes.   Servings: 6
Ingredients:
Salt and pepper
16 oz. chicken ravioli
1 pinch cumin powder
2 cups fresh spinach, shredded
1-can fire roasted tomatoes
1 cup vegetables stock
1 shallot, chopped.
4 garlic cloves, minced.
1/4 tsp. coriander powder.

Directions:
1. Put the garlic, coriander powder, tomatoes, ravioli, shallot, stock, cumin and spinach in your slow cooker.
2. Add salt and pepper and cook for 2½ hours on high settings.
3. Serve the dish warm and fresh.

Creamy Chicken and Mushroom Pot Pie.

Time: 6 hrs. 15 minutes.   Servings: 6
Ingredients:
1/2 tsp. dried thyme
1 sheet puff pastry
1 cup frozen peas
1 cup vegetable stock
4 cups sliced cremini mushrooms
2 chicken breasts, cubed.
1 large onion, chopped.
4 carrots, sliced.
Salt and pepper.

Directions:
1. Put the chicken, onion, peas, mushrooms, carrots, stock, and thyme in your crock pot.
2. Add salt and pepper then top with the puff pastry.
3. Cover and cook for 6 hours on low settings.
4. Serve the pot pie warm.

Lemon Garlic Roasted Chicken

Time: 6 hrs. 15 minutes.   Servings: 6
Ingredients:
1 lemon, sliced.
1 thyme sprig
1 rosemary sprig
6 chicken thighs
6 garlic cloves, chopped.
1/2 cup chicken stock
2 tbsp. butter
Salt and pepper
Directions:
1. Place the chicken in the clean crock pot, then add salt and pepper.
2. Top the chicken with stock, thyme sprig, lemon slices, garlic, butter, and rosemary sprig.
3. Cook for 6 hours on low settings.
4. Serve the chicken warm.

Tarragon Chicken.

Time: 6 hrs. 15 minutes.   Servings: 6

Ingredients:

4 garlic cloves, minced.
1 tsp. lemon zest
Salt and pepper
2 tbsp. chopped parsley for serving
1 tbsp. cornstarch
3-lbs. chicken drumsticks
1/2 cup heavy cream
1/2 cup chicken stock
2 tbsp. Dijon mustard
1 tsp. dried tarragon.

Directions:

1. Put the cream, cornstarch, chicken stock, garlic, chicken, mustard, tarragon, and lemon zest in the crock pot.
2. Add salt and pepper and cook for 6 hours on low settings.
3. Serve the chicken warm and fresh with Parsley.

Italian Fennel Braised Chicken

Time: 6 hrs. 30 minutes.   Servings: 8

Ingredients:

1 tsp. dried basil
1 large fennel bulb, sliced.
1 large onion, sliced.
Salt and pepper
1 rosemary sprig
1 cup chicken stock
2 garlic cloves, chopped.
8 chicken thighs
1-can (15 oz. cannellini beans, drained.
2 yellow bell peppers, cored and sliced
2 ripe tomatoes, peeled and diced.

Directions:

1. Mix the chicken, fennel and the remaining ingredients in the crock pot.
2. Add salt and pepper and cook for 6 hours on low settings.
3. Serve the chicken warm.

Swiss Cheese Saucy Chicken

Time: 3 hrs. 15 minutes.   Servings: 4

Ingredients:

Salt and pepper.
1/2 cup chicken stock
1 cup grated Swiss cheese
1 celery stalk, sliced.
4 boneless chicken breasts
1-can cream of mushrooms soup
1 shallot, sliced.

Directions:

1. Season the chicken with enough salt and pepper.
2. Place the chicken in a clean crock pot and add the remaining ingredients.
3. Cook for 3 hours on high settings.
4. Serve the chicken warm with your favorite dish.

Button Mushroom Chicken Stew

Time: 6 hrs. 15 minutes.   Servings: 6

Ingredients:

1 cup vegetable stock
1 thyme sprig
2 tbsp. canola oil
Salt and pepper
2 garlic cloves, minced.
1 shallot, chopped.
2 chicken breasts, cubed.
4 cups button mushrooms
1 cup cream cheese

Directions:

1. Heat the oil in a clean pan and add the chicken. Cook for about 5 minutes on medium flame until it turns golden brown.
2. Transfer in the slow cooker and add the remaining ingredients.
3. Add salt and pepper and cook for 6 hours on low settings.
4. Serve the chicken stew warm.

Red Salsa Chicken

Time: 8 hrs. 15 minutes.   Servings: 8
Ingredients:
2 cups red salsa
Salt and pepper
1/2 cup chicken stock
8 chicken thighs
1 cup grated Cheddar cheese

Directions:
1. Mix the chicken with the salsa and stock in the slow cooker.
2. Add the cheese, salt and pepper and cook for 8 hours on low settings.
3. Serve the chicken warm.

Caramelized Onions Chicken Stew

Time: 6 hrs. 30 minutes.   Servings: 6
Ingredients:
1 celery stalk, sliced.
2 tbsp. canola oil
2 red bell peppers, cored and sliced
1/4 cup dry white wine
1-can fire roasted tomatoes
1/2 tsp. dried thyme
2 chicken breasts, cubed.
3 large onions, sliced.
4 bacon slices, chopped.
Salt and pepper.

Directions:
1. Heat the oil in a clean pan and add the bacon. Cook until crisp then add the onions.
2. Cook for 10 minutes until the onions are soft.
3. Place in your slow cooker. Add the remaining ingredients and sprinkle with salt and pepper.
4. Cook for 6 hours on low settings.
5. Serve the stew warm.

Mexican Chicken Stew

Time: 8 hrs. 15 minutes.   Servings: 8
Ingredients:
1 tsp. taco seasoning
1/2 tsp. chili powder
Salt and pepper.
1 cup chicken stock
1-can (15 oz. diced tomatoes)
1 cup red salsa
1/2 cup cream cheese
4 chicken breasts, cubed.
1-can (15 oz. black beans, drained).
1-can (10 oz. sweet corn, drained).

Directions:
1. Put the chicken, beans, corn, tomatoes, red salsa, taco seasoning, chili powder, stock, and cream cheese in the slow cooker.
2. Add salt and pepper to taste and cook on low settings for 8 hours.
3. Serve the stew warm.

Whole Orange Glazed Chicken

Time: 2 hrs. 45 minutes.   Servings: 4
Ingredients:
4 chicken thighs
1/2 cup chicken stock
1 large orange, cut into segments
2 tbsp. soy sauce
1 tbsp. honey
1 tsp. hot sauce
1/2 tsp. sesame seeds
Salt and pepper to taste
Cooked white rice for serving
Directions:

1. Put all the necessary ingredients in your crock pot.
2. Cover and cook for 2½ hours on high settings.
3. Serve the chicken warm over cooked white rice.

Cacciatore Chicken

Time: 7 hrs. 15 minutes.   Servings: 8
Ingredients:

1 large onion, sliced.
1/4 cup dry white wine
1 bay leaf
2 cups sliced mushrooms
2 tbsp. tomato paste
1 tbsp. cornstarch
1 tsp. dried basil
2-lbs. chicken drumsticks
1 red bell pepper, cored and sliced
1 yellow bell pepper, cored and sliced
2 garlic cloves, minced.
1 cup chicken stock
2 celery stalks, sliced.
2 carrots, sliced.
2 tbsp. canola oil
1/2 tsp. dried oregano
Salt and pepper.

Directions:

1. Heat the canola oil in a pan. Add the chicken and cook until golden.
2. Place the chicken in the crock pot and add the remaining ingredients.
3. Sprinkle with salt and pepper and cook for 7 hours on low settings.
4. Serve the chicken warm.

Arroz Con Pollo

Time: 6 hrs. 15 minutes.   Servings: 8
Ingredients:

1 cup green peas
1 cup sliced mushrooms
4 chicken breasts, halved
1 rosemary sprig
1 onion, chopped.
Salt and pepper.
2 ripe tomatoes, peeled and diced.
1 cup wild rice
2 cups vegetable stock
1 thyme sprig
2 celery stalks, sliced.
1 red chili, chopped.

Directions:

1. Put the onion, red chili, rice, green peas, celery, tomatoes, mushrooms, stock, and chicken in the crock pot.
2. Add the rosemary, salt, thyme sprig, and pepper and cook for 6 hours on low settings.
3. Serve the dish warm.

Honey Sesame Glazed Chicken

Time: 6 hrs. 15 minutes.   Servings: 4
Ingredients:

2 garlic cloves, minced.
2 tbsp. soy sauce
1/2 tsp. red pepper flakes
1 tsp. grated ginger
1 tsp. sesame oil
2 tbsp. sesame seeds
4 chicken breasts
1/4 cup chicken stock
1/4 cup ketchup
3 tbsp. honey
Salt and pepper to taste

Directions:

1. Put the chicken and the remaining ingredients in the crock pot.
2. Cover and for 6 hours cook on low settings.
3. Serve the chicken warm.

Honey Glazed Chicken Drumsticks

Time: 6 hrs. 15 minutes.   Servings: 6
Ingredients:

2-lbs. chicken drumsticks
2 garlic cloves, minced.
1/4 cup chicken stock
1/4 cup fresh orange juice
2 tbsp. soy sauce
1 tbsp. grated zest
2 tbsp. sesame seeds
1/4 tsp. chili powder
1 tsp. rice vinegar

Directions:

1. Put all the necessary ingredients in your crock pot.
2. Cover and cook for 6 hours on low settings.
3. Serve the chicken warm.

CHAPTER 4

SOUP RECIPES

Free bonus password:

crockbonus4u

Butternut Squash Creamy Soup

Time: 4 1/4 hours   **Servings: 6**

Ingredients:

1 sweet onion, chopped   2 parsnips, cubed
1 potato, peeled and cubed   Salt and pepper
3 cups water   2 cups chicken stock
1 pinch cayenne pepper   1/4 teaspoon cumin powder
2 tablespoons olive oil
2 garlic cloves, chopped
2 cups butternut squash cubed
1 celery root, peeled and cubed

Directions:

1. Heat the oil in a clean pan and add the onion and garlic. Cook for 2-3 minutes until softened then place it in the slow cooker.
2. Add the remaining ingredients and salt and pepper.
3. Cook the soup for 4 hours on low settings.
4. When done, remove the cover and puree the soup with an immersion blender.
5. Serve the soup warm.

Creamy White Bean Soup

Time: 4 1/4 hours   **Servings: 6**

Ingredients:

2 garlic cloves, chopped   1 parsnip, diced
2 cups chicken stock   3 cups water
1/2 teaspoon dried thyme   Salt and pepper
1 tablespoon olive oil
1/2 celery root, peeled and cubed
1 sweet onion, chopped
1 can (15 oz.) white beans, drained

Directions:

1. Heat the oil in a clean pan and add the onion, garlic, celery, and parsnip. Cook for 5 minutes until softened then put the mixture in the slow cooker.
2. Add the remaining necessary ingredients and cook for 4 hours on low settings.
3. When done, puree the soup with an immersion blender and blend until smooth and creamy.
4. Serve the soup warm.

Creamy Bacon Soup

Time: 1 3/4 hours   **Servings: 6**

Ingredients:

1 tablespoon olive oil   6 bacon slices, chopped
1 sweet onion, chopped   1 parsnip, diced
1/2 celery root, cubed   2 cups chicken stock
3 cups water   Salt and pepper
1 1/2 pounds potatoes, peeled and cubed

Directions:

1. Heat the oil in a clean pan, then add the bacon. Cook until soft then transfer the bacon to a plate.
2. Pour the bacon fat in the slow cooker and add the remaining ingredients.
3. Add salt and pepper and cook for 1 1/2 hours on high settings.
4. When done, blend the soup with an immersion blender until smooth.
5. Pour the mixture into a bowl and add bacon.
6. Serve right away.

Pinto Bean Chili Soup

Time: 4 1/4 hours   **Servings: 10**

Ingredients:

2 tablespoons olive oil   1 red onion, chopped
1 garlic clove, chopped   4 cups chicken stock
1/2 teaspoon chili powder   1 bay leaf
1/2 teaspoon cumin powder   Salt and pepper
2 cups butternut squash cubes   1 thyme sprig
2 cups cooked pinto beans   2 cups water
1/2 cup canned sweet corn, drained
2 tablespoons tomato paste
2 red bell peppers, cored and diced

Directions:

1. Heat the oil in a clean pan and add the onion. Cook for 2 minutes until softened.
2. Put the chicken in your slow cooker. Add the chili powder, cumin, bell peppers, garlic, corn, water, stock, tomato paste, bay leaf, butternut squash, pinto beans, and thyme.
3. Add salt and pepper and cook the soup for 4 hours on low settings.
4. Serve the soup warm or cool.

Black Bean Soup

Time: 7 1/4 hours   **Servings: 8**
Ingredients:

1/2 pound black beans, rinsed
1 parsnip, diced
1 red bell peppers, cored and diced
1/2 cup sour cream for serving
2 tablespoons tomato paste
1/2 teaspoon cumin powder
1/4 teaspoon chili powder
1 sweet onion, chopped
2 tablespoons chopped cilantro for serving

Salt and pepper
1 celery stalk, diced
5 cups water
2 tomatoes, diced
1 bay leaf
2 carrots, diced
2 cups chicken stock

Directions:

1. Put the chicken stock, water, black beans, and vegetables in your slow cooker.
2. Add the bay leaf, salt, cumin powder, chili powder, and pepper and cook the soup for 7 hours on low settings.
3. When done, add the cilantro. Pour the soup in bowls, top with sour cream, and then serve.

Posole Soup

Time: 6 1/4 hours   **Servings: 8**
Ingredients:

1 pound pork tenderloin, cubed
1 sweet onion, chopped
1/2 teaspoon cumin powder
1/2 teaspoon dried oregano
1/4 teaspoon chili powder
1 can sweet corn, drained
2 jalapeno peppers, chopped
Salt and pepper
1 can (15 oz.) black beans, drained

2 garlic cloves, chopped
2 cups water
1/2 teaspoon dried basil
1 tablespoons canola oil
1 cup diced tomatoes
4 cups chicken stock
2 limes, juiced

Directions:

1. Heat the canola oil in a clean pan and add the tenderloin. Cook for 5 minutes.
2. Add the pork in the slow cooker and add the remaining ingredients, except the lime juice.
3. Add salt and pepper and cook for 6 hours on low settings.
4. When done, add the lime juice and serve the soup warm.

Three Bean Soup

Time: 4 1/2 hours   **Servings: 10**
Ingredients:

2 tablespoons olive oil
2 garlic cloves, minced
2 cups chicken stock
1 cup diced tomatoes
1 lime, juiced
2 tablespoons chopped parsley
2 red bell peppers, cored and diced
1 can (15 oz.) black beans, drained
1 can (15 oz.) kidney beans, drained
1 can (15 oz.) pinto beans, drained

2 sweet onions, chopped
2 carrots, diced
4 cups water
Salt and pepper
1/2 cup sour cream

Directions:

1. Heat the oil in a clean pan and add the garlic, peppers, onions, and carrot. Cook for 5 minutes.
2. Put the mixture in the slow cooker and add the tomatoes, salt, beans, stock, water, and pepper.
3. Cook for 4 hours on low settings.
4. When done, add the lime juice.
5. Pour the soup in serving bowls and add sour cream and parsley.
6. Serve the soup warm.

Provencal Beef Soup

Time: 7 1/4 hours   **Servings: 8**
Ingredients:

Salt and pepper
1 sweet onion, chopped
1 can diced tomatoes
1 cup beef stock
1 cup red wine
1 garlic clove, chopped
2 carrots, sliced
2 tablespoons olive oil
1 pound beef roast, cubed
1 celery stalk, sliced
4 cups water
1/2 teaspoon dried thyme
1 bay leaf

Directions:

1. Heat the oil in a clean pan and add the beef roast. Cook for a few minutes then put the beef in a slow cooker.
2. Add the remaining ingredients and also salt and pepper.
3. Cook for 7 hours on low settings.
4. Serve the soup warm.

Sausage Bean Soup

Time: 3 1/4 hours   Servings: 8
Ingredients:
2 bacon slices, chopped   1 sweet onion, chopped
1 garlic clove, chopped   1 can diced tomatoes
1/2 teaspoon dried rosemary   4 cups water
4 pork sausages, sliced   1 carrot, diced
1 parsnip, diced   1 celery stalk, sliced
2 cups chicken stock   Salt and pepper
1/2 teaspoon dried thyme
1 can (15 oz.) white beans, drained

Directions:
1. Place a clean pan over medium heat and add the bacon. Sauté for 2-3 minutes until crisp.
2. Place the bacon in your slow cooker.
3. Add the remaining ingredients and also salt and pepper.
4. Cook the soup for 3 hours on high settings.
5. Serve warm.

Curried Lentil Soup

Time: 4 1/4 hours   Servings: 8
Ingredients:
1 teaspoon curry powder
1/4 teaspoon ground ginger
Salt and pepper
1 cup dried lentils, rinsed
1 carrot, diced
1 celery stalk, sliced
1 parsnip, diced
1 cup diced tomatoes
4 bacon slices, chopped
1 sweet onion, chopped
2 garlic cloves, chopped
2 cups chicken stock
4 cups water
1 lime, juiced
2 tablespoons chopped parsley

Directions:
1. Place a clean pan over medium heat and add the bacon. Cook for a few minutes until crisp.
2. Place the bacon in a slow cooker and add the lentils, carrot, water, curry powder, celery, onion, garlic, parsnip, tomatoes, stock, and ginger.
3. Add salt and pepper and cook for 4 hours on low settings.
4. When done, add the lime juice and chopped parsley and serve the soup warm.

Tuscan Chicken Soup

Time: 6 1/4 hours   Servings: 6
Ingredients:
2 chicken breasts, cubed   2 tablespoons canola oil
1 shallot, chopped   1 carrot, diced
1 parsnip, diced   1 celery stalk, sliced
1 can diced tomatoes   2 cups chicken stock
2 cups water   Salt and pepper
1 teaspoon dried Italian herbs   2 oz. Parmesan shavings
1 red bell peppers, cored and diced
1 can (15 oz.) cannellini beans, drained

Directions:
1. Heat the canola oil in a clean pan and add the chicken. Cook for a few minutes until golden brown.
2. Transfer the chicken in your slow cooker.
3. Add the shallot, parsnip, beans, tomatoes, stock, celery, bell peppers, and water.
4. Add salt, pepper, and herbs and cook for 6 hours on low settings.
5. Serve the soup warm, topped with.

Tomato Beef Soup

Time: 8 1/4 hours   Servings: 8
Ingredients:
2 tablespoons olive oil
2 bacon slices, chopped
2 pounds beef roast, cubed
2 sweet onions, chopped
2 tomatoes, peeled and diced
2 cups tomato sauce
1 cup beef stock
3 cups water
Salt and pepper
1 thyme sprig
1 rosemary sprig

Directions:
1. Heat the oil in a clean pan and add the bacon. Cook until crisp and add the beef roast. Cook for 5 minutes.
2. Transfer the beet and bacon in a slow cooker.
3. Add the remaining ingredients and also salt and pepper.
4. Cook for 8 hours on low settings.
5. Serve the soup warm.

Coconut Squash Soup

Time: 2 1/4 hours   **Servings: 6**
Ingredients:

1 tablespoon olive oil	1 shallot, chopped
1/2 teaspoon grated ginger	2 garlic cloves, minced
3 cups butternut squash cubes	2 cups chicken stock
2 cups water	1 cup coconut milk
1 tablespoon tomato paste	Salt and pepper
1 tablespoon curry paste	1 teaspoon brown sugar
1 teaspoon Worcestershire sauce	

Directions:
1. Heat the oil in a clean pan and add the shallot, ginger, garlic, and curry paste. Cook for 1 minute. Place the mixture in a slow cooker.
2. Add the remaining ingredients and also salt and pepper.
3. Cover and cook for 2 hours on high settings.
4. When done, blend the soup with an immersion blender until smooth.
5. Serve it warm.

Creamy Potato Soup

Time: 6 1/2 hours   **Servings: 6**
Ingredients:

6 bacon slices, chopped
1 sweet onion, chopped
1 can condensed chicken soup
6 medium size potatoes, peeled and cubed
2 cups water
Salt and pepper
1 1/2 cups half and half
1 tablespoon chopped parsley

Directions:
1. Place a clean pan over medium heat and add the bacon. Cook until soft then transfer the bacon and its fat in a slow cooker.
2. Add the chicken soup, potatoes, onion, water, salt and pepper and cook for 4 hours on low settings.
3. Add the half and half and continue cooking for another 2 hours.
4. When done, add the chopped parsley and serve the soup warm.

Italian Barley Soup

Time: 6 1/4 hours   **Servings: 6**
Ingredients:

1/2 teaspoon dried thyme	Salt and pepper
1 carrot, sliced	1 parsnip, sliced
1 pound beef roast, cubed	2 tablespoons olive oil
1 large sweet onion, chopped	3 cups water
1/2 cup uncooked barley	2 cups beef stock
1/2 teaspoon dried oregano	1 teaspoon dried basil
2 ripe tomatoes, peeled and diced	

Directions:
1. Heat the oil in a clean pan and add the beef. Cook for 5-6 minutes.
2. Put the beef in a slow cooker and add the remaining ingredients.
3. Add salt and pepper and cook the soup for 6 hours on low settings.
4. Serve the soup warm.

Quick Lentil Ham Soup

Time: 1 3/4 hours   **Servings: 6**
Ingredients:

1 tablespoon olive oil
1/2 cup tomato sauce
1 1/2 cups chicken stock
Salt and pepper
4 oz. ham, diced
1 shallot, chopped
1/2 teaspoon dried oregano
1/2 teaspoon dried basil
1 carrot, diced
1 celery stalk, sliced
1 cup dried lentils, rinsed
2 cups water

Directions:
1. Mix oregano, basil, olive oil, water, tomato sauce, celery, lentils, ham, carrot, shallot, and stock.
2. Add salt and pepper and cook for 1 1/2 hours on high settings.
3. Serve the soup warm or cool.

Split Pea Sausage Soup

Time: 6 1/4 hours   Servings: 8

Ingredients:

2 carrots, diced
2 tablespoons tomato paste
Salt and pepper
1 lemon, juiced
1 celery stalk, diced
1 garlic clove, chopped
2 cups split peas, rinsed
8 cups water
4 Italian sausages, sliced
1 sweet onion, chopped
1 red chili, chopped
1/2 teaspoon dried oregano
2 tablespoons chopped parsley

Directions:

1. Put the celery, garlic, red chili, split peas, onion, carrots, water, sausages, oregano and tomato paste in your slow cooker.
2. Add salt and pepper and cook for 6 hours on low settings.
3. When done, add the lemon juice and parsley
4. Serve the soup warm.

Zucchini Soup

Time: 2 1/4 hours   Servings: 6

Ingredients:

1 pound Italian sausages, sliced
2 celery stalks, sliced
2 zucchinis, cubed
2 large potatoes, peeled and cubed
2 yellow bell peppers, cored and diced
2 carrots, sliced
1 shallot, chopped
3 cups water
2 cups vegetable stock
1/2 teaspoon dried oregano
1/2 teaspoon dried basil
1/4 teaspoon garlic powder
Salt and pepper to taste
2 tablespoons chopped parsley

Directions:

1. Put the zucchinis, potatoes, sausages, celery stalks, shallot, water, bell peppers, carrots, stock, and seasoning in your slow cooker.
2. Add salt and pepper and cook for 2 hours on high settings.
3. When done, add the parsley and serve the soup warm.

Beef Taco Soup

Time: 7 1/4 hours   Servings: 8

Ingredients:

1 pound beef stock, cubed
1 garlic clove, chopped
1 tablespoon olive oil
1 onion, chopped

1 can (15 oz.) black beans, drained
1 can (15 oz.) cannellini beans, drained
1 cup canned corn, drained
2 tablespoons taco seasoning
1 jalapeno pepper, chopped
3 cups water
1 avocado, sliced
1 cup tomato sauce
1 cup dark beer
Salt and pepper
2 cups beef stock
1/2 cup sour cream

Directions:

1. Heat the oil in a clean pan and add the onion, beef, and garlic. Cook for 2 minutes then place in a slow cooker.
2. Add the tomato sauce, beer, beans, corn, taco seasoning, and jalapeno.
3. Add salt and pepper and cook for 7 hours on low settings.
4. Pour the soup into serving bowls and add sour cream and avocado slices.

Spicy Black Bean Soup

Time: 6 1/4 hours   Servings: 6

Ingredients:

1/2 cup diced tomatoes
Salt and pepper
2 jalapeno peppers, chopped
2 cups chicken stock
1 can (15 oz.) black beans, drained
1/2 teaspoon cumin powder
1/2 cup sour cream
4 cups water
1 tablespoon olive oil
1 shallot, chopped
1 carrot, diced
1/2 teaspoon chili powder

Directions:

1. Put the carrot, jalapeno peppers, olive oil, shallot, stock, beans, water, and spices in a slow cooker.
2. Add salt and pepper and cook for 6 hours on low settings.
3. Serve the soup warm, topped with sour cream.

Chicken Sausage Soup

Time: 6 1/2 hours   **Servings: 8**
Ingredients:

1 sweet onion, chopped	1 carrot, diced
2 garlic cloves, chopped	1 can cannellini beans
1/2 teaspoon dried basil	1 can diced tomatoes
1/4 cup dry white wine	2 cups chicken stock
1/2 cup short pasta	Salt and pepper
2 tablespoons chopped parsley	3 cups water
1 red bell pepper, cored and diced	
1/2 teaspoon dried oregano	
1 pound Italian sausages, sliced	

Directions:

1. Put the oregano, basil, tomatoes, garlic, bell pepper, sausages, onion, carrot, salt, pepper, beans, wine, stock and water in a slow cooker.
2. Cook for 1 hour on high settings then add the pasta and continue cooking for another 5 hours.
3. Serve the soup warm with freshly chopped parsley.

Beef Cabbage Soup

Time: 7 1/2 hours   **Servings: 8**
Ingredients:
1/2 teaspoon cumin seeds
Salt and pepper
1 sweet onion, chopped
1 carrot, grated
1 small cabbage head, shredded
1 pound beef roast, cubed
2 tablespoons olive oil
1 can (15 oz.) diced tomatoes
2 cups beef stock
2 cups water

Directions:

1. Heat the oil in a clean pan and add the beef roast. Cook for 5-6 minutes then transfer the meat in a slow cooker.
2. Add the remaining ingredients and also salt and pepper.
3. Cook for 7 hours on low settings.
4. Serve the cabbage soup warm.

Beef Vegetable Soup

Time: 7 1/4 hours   **Servings: 8**
Ingredients:
1 carrot, sliced
1 garlic clove, chopped
1/2 head cauliflower, cut into florets
4 cups water
Salt and pepper
1 pound beef roast, cubed
2 large potatoes, peeled and cubed
1 cup diced tomatoes
1/2 teaspoon dried basil
2 cups beef stock
2 tablespoons canola oil
1 celery stalk, sliced
1 sweet onion, chopped

Directions:

1. Heat the oil in a clean pan and add the beef. Cook for a few minutes then place the beef in a slow cooker.
2. Add the remaining ingredients and also salt and pepper.
3. Cover and cook for 7 hours on low settings.
4. Serve it warm.

Sweet Corn Chowder

Time: 6 1/4 hours   **Servings: 8**
Ingredients:
2 shallots, chopped
2 cups chicken stock
2 cups water
Salt and pepper
1 can (15 oz.) sweet corn, drained
4 medium size potatoes, peeled and cubed
1 celery stalk, sliced

Directions

1. Put the celery, corn, shallot, potatoes, stock, and water in a slow cooker.
2. Add salt and pepper and cook for 6 hours on low settings.
3. When done, remove a few tablespoons of corn from the pot then puree the rest of the soup in the pot.
4. Pour the soup into serving bowls and add the reserved corn.
5. Serve warm.

Chicken Enchilada Soup

Time: 6 1/2 hours   Servings: 8
Ingredients:
1 bay leaf
Salt and pepper
2 garlic cloves, chopped
1 chicken breast, diced
1 can (15 oz.) diced tomatoes
1 tablespoon olive oil
2 shallots, chopped
4 cups water
1/2 teaspoon cumin powder
1/2 teaspoon chili powder
1 can (15 oz.) sweet corn, drained
1 can (4 oz.) green chile, chopped
2 cups chicken stock

Directions:
1. Put the garlic, olive oil, shallots, and chicken in a pan and cook for 5 minutes.
2. Put the chicken in your slow cooker and add the remaining ingredients.
3. Add salt and pepper and cook for 6 hours on low settings.
4. Serve the soup warm.

Ham Bone Cabbage Soup

Time: 7 1/4 hours   Servings: 8
Ingredients:
1 mediums size cabbage head, shredded
2 tablespoons tomato paste
1 can diced tomatoes
1 thyme sprig
1 lemon, juiced
1 ham bone
1 sweet onion, chopped
2 cups beef stock
Salt and pepper
1 bay leaf

Directions:
1. Put the stock, bay leaf, cabbage, tomato paste, ham bone, onion, tomatoes, and thyme sprig in your slow cooker.
2. Add salt and pepper and cook for 7 hours on low settings.
3. When done, add the lemon juice
4. Serve the soup warm.

Italian Barley Soup

Time: 6 1/4 hours   Servings: 8
Ingredients:
2 tablespoons olive oil   1 shallot, chopped
1 garlic clove, chopped   1 carrot, diced
1 celery stalk, diced   3 cups water
2 cups vegetable stock   2/3 cup pearl barley
1 teaspoon dried oregano   1 teaspoon dried basil
1 lemon, juiced   Salt and pepper
2 red bell peppers, cored and diced
2 tomatoes, peeled and diced
2 cups fresh spinach, chopped

Directions:
1. Heat the oil in a clean pan and add the shallot, garlic, carrot and celery, and also bell peppers.
2. Cook for 5 minutes just until softened then place in a slow cooker.
3. Add the remaining ingredients and also salt and pepper.
4. Cook for 6 hours on low settings.
5. Serve the soup warm.

Lima Bean Soup

Time: 7 1/4 hours   Servings: 8
Ingredients:
2 carrots, diced
2 potatoes, peeled and cubed
1 celery stalk, sliced
2 bacon slices, chopped
4 cups frozen lima beans
3 cups water
1 bay leaf
2 shallots, chopped
Salt and pepper
1 can diced tomatoes
2 cups vegetable stock
1 tablespoon chopped cilantro

Directions:
1. Put the shallots, potatoes, celery, carrots, bacon, lima beans, and tomatoes in a slow cooker.
2. Add the remaining necessary ingredients, except cilantro and sprinkle with salt and pepper.
3. Cook for 7 hours on low settings.
4. When done, add the chopped cilantro
5. Serve the soup warm.

Okra Vegetable Soup

Time: 7 1/4 hours **Servings: 8**

Ingredients:

1 pound ground beef
2 tablespoons canola oil
2 shallots, chopped
1 carrot, sliced
1 can fire roasted tomatoes, chopped
2 cups chopped okra
1/2 cup green peas
2 potatoes, peeled and cubed
1/2 cup sweet corn, drained
Salt and pepper to taste
2 cups water
2 cups chicken stock
1 lemon, juiced

Directions:

1. Heat the oil in a clean pan and add the beef. Cook for a few minutes then place the meat in a slow cooker.
2. Add the corn, water, tomatoes, okra, shallots, carrot, peas, potatoes, and stock, as well as lemon juice, salt, and pepper.
3. Cook the soup for 7 hours on low settings.
4. Serve the soup warm.

Mexican Beef Soup

Time: 8 1/4 hours **Servings: 6**

Ingredients:

1/2 cup red salsa
1 chipotle pepper, chopped
Salt and pepper to taste
1 pound ground beef
1 sweet onion, chopped
2 cups beef stock
1 can (15 oz.) diced tomatoes
2 tablespoons canola oil
2 red bell peppers, cored and diced
1 can (15 oz.) black beans, drained
3 cups water

Directions:

1. Heat the oil in a clean pan and add the beef. Cook for 5 minutes, stirring often, then transfer the beef in your slow cooker.
2. Add the remaining ingredients and adjust the taste with salt and pepper.
3. Cook on low settings for 8 hours.
4. Serve the soup warm or chilled.

Hungarian Borscht

Time: 8 1/4 hours **Servings: 8**

Ingredients:

1 pound beef roast, cubed
2 potatoes, peeled and cubed
2 tablespoons tomato paste
4 cups water
1/2 teaspoon cumin seeds
1 teaspoon red wine vinegar
1 teaspoon honey
4 medium size beets, peeled and cubed
2 tablespoons canola oil
1 sweet onion, chopped
Salt and pepper
1 cup vegetable stock
1 can diced tomatoes
1 teaspoon dried parsley
1/2 teaspoon dried dill

Directions:

1. Heat the oil in a clean pan and add the beef. Cook for a few minutes until golden.
2. Place the meat in a slow cooker and add the potatoes, onion, beets, tomatoes, and tomato paste.
3. Add salt and pepper, as well as the remaining ingredients and cook on low settings for 8 hours.
4. Serve the soup warm or chilled.

Chicken Rice Soup

Time: 7 1/4 hours **Servings: 8**

Ingredients:

2 tablespoons canola oil
2/3 cup white rice, rinsed
Salt and pepper
2 chicken breasts, cubed
2 carrots, diced
2 red bell peppers, cored and diced
1 can diced tomatoes
2 cups water
2 cups chicken stock
1 celery stalk, sliced
1 sweet onion, chopped
1 parsnip, diced

Directions:

1. Heat the canola oil in a clean pan and add the chicken. Cook for 5 minutes until golden.
2. Transfer the golden chicken to a slow cooker and add the remaining ingredients.
3. Add salt and pepper and cook for 7 hours on low settings.
4. Serve the soup warm.

Ham Potato Chowder

Time: 4 1/4 hours　　　　**Servings: 8**

Ingredients:

1 cup sweet corn, drained
1/2 teaspoon celery seeds
1 can condensed chicken soup
2 cups water
4 potatoes, peeled and cubed
1 sweet onion, chopped
1 tablespoon olive oil
Salt and pepper
1 cup diced ham
1/2 teaspoon cumin seeds

Directions:

1. Combine the chicken soup, onion, water, potatoes, olive oil, ham, and corn in a slow cooker.
2. Add the celery seeds and cumin seeds and sprinkle with salt and pepper.
3. Cook for 4 hours on high settings.
4. Serve the soup warm.

Potato Kielbasa Soup

Time: 6 1/4 hours　　　　**Servings: 8**

Ingredients:

1 parsnip, diced
1 garlic clove, chopped
1 pound kielbasa sausages, sliced
1 sweet onion, chopped
2 carrots, diced
2 red bell peppers, cored and diced
2 large potatoes, peeled and cubed
Salt and pepper to taste
2 cups chicken stock
3 cups water
1/2 pound fresh spinach, shredded
1 lemon, juiced

Directions:

1. Combine the sausages, garlic, potatoes, onion, carrots, parsnip, and bell peppers in a slow cooker.
2. Add the spinach, stock, water, and lemon juice then add salt and pepper.
3. Cook for 6 hours on low settings.
4. Serve the soup warm.

Curried Corn Chowder

Time: 8 1/4 hours　　　　**Servings: 8**

Ingredients:

1 can (15 oz.) sweet corn, drained
1 1/2 cups whole milk
Salt and pepper
2 large potatoes, peeled and cubed
1 sweet onion, chopped
2 garlic cloves, chopped
2 cups chicken stock
1/2 chili pepper, chopped
1/4 teaspoon cumin seeds

Directions:

1. Mix the sweet corn, potatoes, onion, garlic, stock, and chili pepper in your slow cooker.
2. Add the remaining ingredients and sprinkle with salt and pepper.
3. Cook for 8 hours on low settings.
4. Serve the soup warm.

Two-Fish Soup

Time: 6 1/4 hours　　　　**Servings: 8**

Ingredients:

3 salmon fillets, cubed
3 cod fillets, cubed
2 tablespoons chopped parsley
1 red bell pepper, cored and diced
1 chipotle pepper, chopped
1 carrot, diced
Salt and pepper
1 tablespoon canola oil
1 sweet onion, chopped
1 celery stalk, diced
1 cup diced tomatoes
1 lemon, juiced

Directions:

1. Heat the canola oil in a clean pan and add the onion. Cook for 2 minutes until softened.
2. Place the onion in a slow cooker and add the remaining ingredients.
3. Add salt and pepper and cook for 6 hours on low settings.
4. Serve the soup warm.

Creamy Cauliflower Soup

Time: 3 1/4 hours　　　　　　　**Servings: 6**

Ingredients:
Salt and pepper
1/2 cup water
1 head cauliflower, cut into florets
2 medium size potatoes, peeled and cubed
1 tablespoon canola oil
1 sweet onion, chopped
2 garlic cloves, chopped
1 can condensed cream of chicken soup
1/2 cup grated Parmesan cheese

Directions:
1. Heat the oil in a clean pan and add the onion. Cook for 2 minutes then transfer the onion in your slow cooker.
2. Add the remaining necessary ingredients, except the cheese, and season with salt and pepper.
3. Cook on high settings for 3 hours.
4. When done, puree the soup with an immersion blender.
5. Serve the soup warm.

Winter Veggie Soup

Time: 6 1/2 hours　　　　　　　**Servings: 8**

Ingredients:
1 celery stalk, sliced
1/2 head cabbage, shredded
1 parsnip, sliced
1 sweet onion, chopped
2 carrots, sliced
1 celery root, peeled and cubed
Salt and pepper
1/4 cup white rice, rinsed
1 lemon, juiced
2 cups vegetable stock
3 cups water
1 cup diced tomatoes

Directions:
1. Add the onion, water, tomatoes, carrots, celery stalk, cabbage, parsnip, lemon, celery root, stock, and rice in your slow cooker.
2. Add salt and pepper and also the rice and cook for 6 hours on low settings.
3. Serve the soup warm.

Spiced Creamy Pumpkin Soup

Time: 5 1/4 hours　　　　　　　**Servings: 6**

Ingredients:
1 thyme sprig　　　　　　　Salt and pepper
1/2 cinnamon stick　　　　　1 star anise
2 cups chicken stock　　　　2 carrots, sliced
1/2 teaspoon cumin powder　2 tablespoons olive oil
1/4 teaspoon chili powder　　1 shallot, chopped
2 garlic cloves, chopped　　　2 cups water
1 medium sugar pumpkin, peeled and cubed

Directions:
1. Mix the carrots, garlic, shallot, and olive oil in a pan. Cook for 5 minutes until softened.
2. Place the mixture in a slow cooker and add the remaining ingredients, including the spices.
3. Cook for 5 hours on low settings then remove the thyme sprig, cinnamon, and star anise and puree the soup with an immersion blender.
4. Serve the soup warm.

Kielbasa Kale Soup

Time: 6 1/4 hours　　　　　　　**Servings: 8**

Ingredients:
1 cup diced tomatoes
1 pound kielbasa sausages, sliced
1/2 pound kale, shredded
2 cups chicken stock
2 cups water
Salt and pepper
1 sweet onion, chopped
1 parsnip, diced
1 red bell pepper, cored and diced
1 can (15 oz.) white beans, drained
1 carrot, diced
1/2 teaspoon dried oregano
1/2 teaspoon dried basil

Directions:
1. Put the carrot, parsnip, kielbasa sausages, onion, bell pepper, white beans, tomatoes and kale in a slow cooker.
2. Add the remaining ingredients and also salt and pepper.
3. Cook for 6 hours on low settings.
4. Serve the soup warm or cool.

Lemony Salmon Soup

Time: 4 1/4 hours   **Servings: 6**

Ingredients:

1 shallot, chopped
1 celery stalk, sliced
1 teaspoon lemon zest
1/2 teaspoon dried oregano
2 cups water
1 pound salmon fillets, cubed
1 red bell pepper, cored and diced
1/2 teaspoon dried basil
1 garlic clove, chopped
1 carrot, sliced
1 parsnip, sliced
2 cups milk
1 lemon, juiced
Salt and pepper

Directions:

1. Put the shallot, carrot, parsnip, garlic, celery, and bell pepper in a slow cooker.
2. Add the water, lemon juice, dried herbs, milk, and lemon zest and cook for 1 hour on high settings.
3. Add the fish and also salt and pepper.
4. Cook for 3 extra hours on low settings.
5. Serve the soup warm or cool.

Creamy Noodle Soup

Time: 8 1/4 hours   **Servings: 8**

Ingredients:

2 shallots, chopped
1 celery stalk, sliced
1 cup green peas
6 oz. egg noodles
2 cups water
2 cups chicken stock
1 can condensed chicken soup
2 chicken breasts, cubed
2 tablespoons all-purpose flour
Salt and pepper

Directions:

1. Coat the chicken with salt, pepper and flour and place it in your slow cooker.
2. Add the remaining ingredients and sprinkle with salt and pepper.
3. Cover and cook for 8 hours on low settings.
4. Serve the soup warm.

Asparagus Crab Soup

Time: 2 1/4 hours   **Servings: 6**

Ingredients:

1 tablespoon olive oil
1 shallot, chopped
1 celery stalk, sliced
1 bunch asparagus, trimmed and chopped
1 cup green peas
1 cup chicken stock
2 cups water
Salt and pepper to taste
1 can crab meat, drained

Directions:

1. Heat the oil in a clean pan and add the shallot and celery. Cook for 2 minutes until softened then place in a slow cooker.
2. Add the green peas, stock, asparagus, and water and season with salt and pepper.
3. Cook for 2 hours. on high settings.
4. When done, puree the soup with an immersion blender until creamy.
5. Pour the dish into serving bowls and top with crab meat.

Chunky Potato Ham Soup

Time: 8 1/2 hours   **Servings: 8**

Ingredients:

1 leek, sliced
2 cups chicken stock
3 cups water
Salt and pepper
1 celery stalk, sliced
2 carrots, sliced
2 cups diced ham
1 sweet onion, chopped
1 garlic clove, chopped
2 pounds potatoes, peeled and cubed
1/2 teaspoon dried oregano
1/2 teaspoon dried basil

Directions:

1. Put all the necessary ingredients in a slow cooker.
2. Add salt and pepper and cook for 8 hours on low settings.
3. Serve the soup warm or cool.

Leek Potato Soup

Time: 6 1/2 hours   **Servings: 8**
Ingredients:

4 leeks, sliced
4 bacon slices, chopped
2 cups chicken stock
1 bay leaf
1 thyme sprig
1/4 teaspoon cayenne pepper
1/4 teaspoon smoked paprika
4 large potatoes, peeled and cubed

1 tablespoon olive oil
1 celery stalk, sliced
3 cups water
Salt and pepper
1 rosemary sprig

Directions:

1. Heat the oil in a clean pan and add the bacon. Cook until crisp then add the leeks.
2. Cook for 5 minutes until softened then transfer in your slow cooker.
3. Add the remaining ingredients and cook for about 6 hours on low settings.
4. Serve the soup warm.

Creamy Leek and Potato Soup

Time: 6 1/4 hours   **Servings: 6**
Ingredients:

1 tablespoon all-purpose flour
Salt and pepper
1/2 cup heavy cream
2 cups chicken stock
2 tablespoons olive oil
2 leeks, sliced
2 cups water
4 large potatoes, peeled and cubed
1 thyme sprig

Directions:

1. Heat the oil in a clean pan and add the leeks. Cook for 5 minutes until softened. Add the flour and cook for another 1 minute.
2. Place the mixture in a slow cooker and add the remaining ingredients, except the cream.
3. Cook for 6 hours on low settings.
4. When done, remove the thyme sprig, add the cream and puree the soup with an immersion blender.
5. Serve the soup warm or cool.

Minestrone Soup

Time: 6 1/4 hours   **Servings: 8**
Ingredients:

2 cups water
2 carrots, diced
1 sweet onion, chopped
1 cup frozen green peas
1 teaspoon dried oregano
1 can red beans, drained
1 cup small pasta
2 tablespoons chopped parsley
4 ripe tomatoes, peeled and diced
2 tablespoons tomato paste
4 sun-dried tomatoes, chopped
Grated Parmesan for serving
2 garlic cloves, chopped

4 cups vegetable stock
2 celery stalks, diced
1 zucchini, cubed

1 thyme sprig
1 bay leaf
Salt and pepper

Directions:

1. Put the tomatoes, tomato paste and the remaining ingredients, except chopped parsley, in a slow cooker.
2. Add salt and pepper and cook the soup for 6 hours on low settings.
3. Serve the soup warm and top with chopped parsley and grated Parmesan.

Roasted Bell Pepper Quinoa Soup

Time: 6 1/2 hours   **Servings: 6**
Ingredients:

1 shallot, chopped
1 pinch cayenne pepper
Salt and pepper
1 garlic clove, chopped
4 roasted red bell peppers, chopped
1/2 cup red quinoa, rinsed
1/2 teaspoon dried oregano
1/2 teaspoon dried basil
1/2 cup tomato paste
2 cups vegetable stock
1 cup water

Directions:

1. Put the shallot, tomato paste, stock, garlic, bell peppers, and water in your slow cooker.
2. Add the quinoa, herbs and spices, and also salt and pepper and cover.
3. Cook for 6 hours on low settings.
4. Serve the soup warm.

Red Chili Quinoa Soup

Time: 3 1/4 hours   **Servings: 8**

Ingredients:

Salt and pepper
1/2 teaspoon chili powder
1/2 celery root, peeled and diced
1 can diced tomatoes
1/2 cup quinoa, rinsed
2 shallots, chopped
Sour cream for serving
1 carrot, diced
1 can (15 oz.) red beans, drained
2 cups water
2 cups chicken stock
2 tablespoons chopped cilantro for serving.

Directions:

1. Put the carrot, celery, shallots, and diced tomatoes in your slow cooker.
2. Add the quinoa, water, stock, red beans, and chili powder and sprinkle with salt and pepper.
3. Cook for 3 hours on high settings.
4. Serve the soup warm, topped with cilantro and sour cream.

Corn and Red Pepper Chowder

Time: 8 1/4 hours   **Servings: 8**

Ingredients:

1/4 teaspoon smoked paprika
1/4 teaspoon cumin powder
2 cups water
Salt and pepper
2 tablespoons olive oil
2 large potatoes, peeled and cubed
2 cups frozen sweet corn
2 cups chicken stock
1 shallot, chopped
1 red bell pepper, cored and diced

Directions:

1. Heat the oil in a clean pan and stir in the shallot. Cook until softened then place in your slow cooker.
2. Add the remaining ingredients and also salt and pepper.
3. Cook for 8 hours on low settings.
4. When done, puree the soup in a blender
5. Serve it warm.

Chunky Mushroom Soup

Time: 8 1/2 hours   **Servings: 8**

Ingredients:

2 tablespoons olive oil
1-pound fresh mushrooms, chopped
1 zucchini, cubed
1 sweet onion, chopped
1 garlic clove, chopped
1 yellow bell pepper, cored and diced
3 cups water
1/2 cup tomato sauce
Salt and pepper
2 large potatoes, peeled and cubed
2 tomatoes, peeled and diced
2 cups vegetable stock
1 lemon, juiced
1 tablespoon chopped dill

Directions:

1. Heat the oil in a clean pan and add the onion, garlic, and bell pepper. Cook for 5 mins until softened then place in a slow cooker.
2. Add the mushrooms, stock, water, zucchini, potatoes, tomatoes, and tomato sauce then sprinkle with salt and pepper.
3. Cook on low settings for 8 hours.
4. Add the lemon juice and chopped dill and serve the soup warm.

Chunky Pumpkin and Kale Soup

Time: 6 1/2 hours   **Servings: 6**

Ingredients:

1/2 teaspoon cumin seeds
Salt and pepper
1/2 red chili, chopped
2 tablespoons olive oil
2 cups pumpkin cubes
2 cups vegetable stock
1 sweet onion, chopped
1 red bell pepper, cored and diced
2 cups water
1 bunch kale, shredded

Directions:

1. Put the chili, onion, bell pepper, and olive oil in a slow cooker.
2. Add the remaining ingredients and also salt and pepper.
3. Mix gently then cook for 6 hours on low settings.
4. Serve the soup warm.

White Chicken Chili Soup

Time: 7 1/2 hours   **Servings: 8**
Ingredients:
1/2 teaspoon chili powder
Salt and pepper
1 yellow bell pepper, cored and diced
2 carrots, diced
1 celery stalk, diced
1 pound ground chicken
2 tablespoons olive oil
2 cups chicken stock
3 cups water
1 parsnip, diced
2 cans (15 oz.) white beans, drained

Directions:
1. Heat the oil in a clean pan and add the chicken. Cook for 5 minutes, stirring often, then place the meat in a slow cooker.
2. Add the remaining ingredients and sprinkle with salt and pepper.
3. Cover and cook for 7 hours on low settings.
4. Serve the soup either warm or cool.

Garam Masala Chicken Soup

Time: 8 1/4 hours   **Servings: 8**
Ingredients:
1/2 lemongrass stalk, crushed
1/2 teaspoon cumin seeds
Salt and pepper
1 sweet onion, chopped
1 cup tomato sauce
1 bay leaf
2 garlic cloves, chopped
8 chicken drumsticks
2 tablespoons canola oil
1 teaspoon garam masala
1-pound potatoes, peeled and cubed
1 cup coconut milk
2 cups chicken stock
2 cups water

Directions:
1. Heat the canola oil in a clean pan and add the chicken drumsticks. Cook until golden brown and crusty then place in a slow cooker.
2. Add the remaining ingredients then sprinkle with salt and pepper.
3. Cook for 8 hours on low settings.
4. Serve the soup warm or cool.

Orange Salmon Soup

Time: 2 1/4 hours   **Servings: 8**
Ingredients:
1 lemon, juiced
1 orange, juiced
1/2 teaspoon grated orange zest
Salt and pepper
1 small fennel bulb, sliced
1 cup diced tomatoes
3 salmon fillets, cubed
2 cups vegetable stock
1 sweet onion, chopped
1 garlic clove, chopped
1 celery stalk, sliced
3 cups water

Directions:
1. Mix the celery, fennel bulb, onion, garlic, tomatoes, salmon, stock and water in your slow cooker.
2. Add the remaining ingredients and sprinkle with salt and pepper.
3. Cook for 2 hours on high settings.
4. Serve the soup warm or cool.

Creamy Tortellini Soup

Time: 6 1/4 hours   **Servings: 6**
Ingredients:
1 shallot, chopped
1 garlic clove, chopped
1/2 pound mushrooms, sliced
1 can condensed cream of mushroom soup
2 cups chicken stock
1 cup water
1/2 teaspoon dried oregano
1/2 teaspoon dried basil
1 cup evaporated milk
7 oz. cheese tortellini
Salt and pepper to taste

Directions:
1. Mix the mushrooms, cream of mushroom soup, shallot, garlic, stock, water, dried herbs and milk in your slow cooker.
2. Add the cheese tortellini and sprinkle with salt and pepper.
3. Cook for 6 hours on low settings.
4. Serve the soup warm.

Spicy Chili Soup with Tomatillos

Time: 8 1/2 hours   Servings: 8
Ingredients:
1 jalapeno pepper, chopped
1 can (15 oz.) black beans, drained
1 can fire roasted tomatoes
1/2 pound beef roast, cubed
10 oz. canned tomatillos, rinsed, drained and chopped
1 dried ancho chili, seeded and chopped
1 cup beef stock
4 cups water
Chopped cilantro and sour cream for serving
Salt and pepper
1 bay leaf
1 thyme sprig

Directions:
1. Mix the ancho chili, jalapeno pepper, beef roast, tomatillos, and black beans in your slow cooker.
2. Add the water, salt, tomatoes, beef stock, and pepper, and also bay leaf and thyme sprig.
3. Cook for 8 hours on low settings.
4. Serve the soup warm and also topped with chopped cilantro and a dollop of sour cream.

Portobello Mushroom Soup

Time: 6 1/4 hours   Servings: 6
Ingredients:
4 Portobello mushrooms, sliced
1 shallot, chopped
2 garlic cloves, chopped
1 cup diced tomatoes
1 tablespoon tomato paste
2 cups chicken stock
1 can condensed cream of mushroom soup
Salt and pepper
1/2 teaspoon cumin seeds
1 tablespoon chopped parsley
1 tablespoon chopped cilantro

Directions:
1. Mix the garlic, tomatoes, mushrooms, shallot, tomato paste, stock, and mushroom soup in a slow cooker.
2. Add the cumin seeds then sprinkle with salt and pepper.
3. Cook for 6 hours on low settings.
4. When done, add the chopped parsley and cilantro.
5. Serve the soup warm.

Bouillabaisse Soup

Time: 6 1/2 hours   Servings: 8
Ingredients:
1 pound haddock fillets, cubed
1 tablespoon chopped parsley
2 cups vegetable stock
1 cup diced tomatoes
2 garlic cloves, chopped
1 red bell pepper, cored and diced
2 large potatoes, peeled and cubed
1 celery stalk, sliced
1 carrot, diced
1 fennel bulb, sliced
Salt and pepper
1 shallot, chopped
1/2 lemon, juiced

Directions:
1. Mix the bell pepper, carrot, shallot, garlic, fennel, tomatoes and stock in your slow cooker.
2. Add the lemon juice, salt, potatoes, celery, and pepper and cook on high settings for 1 hour.
3. Add the haddock fillets and continue cooking for 5 minutes on low settings.
4. Serve the soup warm and top with chopped parsley.

Pork and Corn Soup

Time: 8 1/4 hours   Servings: 8
Ingredients:
2 carrots, sliced
2 cups chicken stock
4 cups water
Salt and pepper
2 tablespoons chopped cilantro
1 celery stalk, sliced
2 yellow bell peppers, cored and diced
2 cups frozen sweet corn
1 pound pork roast, cubed
1 sweet onion, chopped
2 bacon slices, chopped
1 garlic clove, chopped
1/2 teaspoon cumin seeds
1/2 red chili, sliced

Directions:
1. Put the bacon, pork roast, sweet onion, and garlic in a pan and cook for 5 minutes, stirring throughout the period.
2. Place in the slow cooker and add the bell peppers, stock, water, sweet corn, cumin seeds, carrots, celery, red chili, salt and pepper.
3. Cook for 8 hours on low settings.
4. When done, add the chopped cilantro.
5. Serve the soup warm.

CHAPTER 5
DESSERT RECIPES

Lavender Blackberry Crumble

Time: 2 1/4 hours   **Servings: 6**
Ingredients:
1 teaspoon dried lavender buds
1 cup all-purpose flour
1 pinch salt
1 1/2 pounds fresh blackberries
2 tablespoons cornstarch
1 teaspoon vanilla extract
1/4 cup white sugar
1/2 cup butter, chilled and cubed

Directions:
1. Combine the vanilla, sugar, blackberries, cornstarch, and lavender in a slow cooker.
2. Mix the salt, flour, and butter in a bowl and rub them well with your fingertips until the mixture looks grainy.
3. Spread the mixture over the veggies and cook for 2 hours on high settings.
4. Serve the crumble cool.

Raspberry Brownie Cake

Time: 3 1/4 hours   **Servings: 10**
Ingredients:
1 cup sugar
4 eggs
1 pinch salt
1/2 cup cocoa powder
1 1/2 cups fresh raspberries
1/2 cup all-purpose flour
1 cup butter, cubed
1 1/2 cups dark chocolate, chopped

Directions:
1. Mix the butter with chocolate in a bowl and place over a hot water bath
2. Melt them together until smooth.
3. Take the bowl from heat and add the sugar and eggs.
4. Add the flour, cocoa powder, and salt, and pour the batter into your greased crock pot.
5. Top with raspberries and cover the pot.
6. Cook for 3 hours on high settings.
7. Allow the cake to cool before serving.

Apple Butter

Time: 8 1/4 hours   **Servings: 12**
Ingredients:
1 cup sugar
4 eggs
1 pinch salt
4 pounds Granny Smith apples, peeled and cored
2 pounds tart apples, peeled and cored
2 cups white sugar
1 cup fresh apple juice
1 teaspoon cinnamon powder
1/2 teaspoon ground ginger

Directions:
1. Mix all the necessary ingredients in a slow cooker and mix properly.
2. Cover and cook on 8 hours.
3. When done, puree the mixture with a blender and pour it into jars.
4. Seal the jars and store them for up to a few months in your storage room.

Pineapple Upside Down Cake

Time: 5 1/4 hours   **Servings: 10**
Ingredients:
1 cup butter, softened
1/2 cup light brown sugar
1/2 teaspoon cinnamon powder
2 tablespoons butter to grease the pot
1 can pineapple chunks, drained
1/2 cup white sugar
2 eggs
1 cup all-purpose flour
1/2 cup ground almonds
1 teaspoon baking powder
1/4 teaspoon salt

Directions:
1. Grease the pot with butter then put the pineapple chunks in the pot.
2. For the cake, mix the softened butter, brown sugar and white sugar in a bowl. Add the eggs and mix.
3. Add the flour, almonds, baking powder and salt, as well as cinnamon.
4. Pour the mixture over the pineapple and bake for 5 hours on low settings.

Pure Berry Crumble

Time: 5 1/4 hours   **Servings: 8**

Ingredients:
1 teaspoon lemon zest
1 cup all-purpose flour
1 pound fresh mixed berries
1 tablespoon cornstarch
1/4 cup white sugar
1/2 teaspoon baking powder
1/2 cup butter, chilled and cubed
1/4 cup cornstarch
1 pinch salt
2 tablespoons sugar

Directions:
1. In the crock pot, combine the berries, cornstarch, 1/4 cup sugar, and lemon zest.
2. In a bowl, add the flour, cornstarch, salt, and baking powder for the topping. When the mixture becomes grainy, add the butter and stir thoroughly.
3. Cover the berries with the mixture, and cook on low settings for 5 hours.
4. Cool the crumble before serving.

Apple Sour Cream Crostata

Time: 6 1/2 hours   **Servings: 8**

Ingredients:
1/4 cup light brown sugar
1 1/2 cups all-purpose flour
1/2 cup butter, chilled and cubed
2 pounds Granny Smith apples, peeled, cored and sliced
1 tablespoon cornstarch
1 teaspoon cinnamon powder
1 pinch salt
2 tablespoons white sugar
1/2 cup sour cream

Directions:
1. In a bowl, combine the butter, flour, white sugar, and salt. Rub the mixture well with your hands until it becomes gritty, then add the sour cream and knead it.
2. To make the dough fit your crock pot, roll it out on a surface dusted with flour.
3. Place the dough into the slow cooker.
4. To make the topping, combine the apples with cornstarch, cinnamon, and light brown sugar. Put the mixture on top of the dough.
5. Put the lid on the pot and cook on low setting for six hours.
6. Serve the crostata cool.

Cranberry Stuffed Apples

Time: 4 1/4 hours   **Servings: 4**

Ingredients:
1/4 cup ground almonds
1/4 cup pecans, chopped
4 large Granny Smith apples
1/2 cup dried cranberries
2 tablespoons honey
1/4 teaspoon cinnamon powder
1/2 cup apple cider

Directions:
1. Each apple should have its core carefully removed before being placed in the slow cooker.
2. In a bowl, combine the cranberries, honey, almonds, pecans, and cinnamon.
3. After adding the apple cider, stuff the apples with this mixture.
4. Cook for 4 hours on low heat with the lid on.
5. Warm apple servings are preferred.

Autumnal Bread Pudding

Time: 5 1/2 hours   **Servings: 8**

Ingredients:
16 oz. bread cubes
2 red apples, peeled and diced
2 pears, peeled and diced
1/2 cup golden raisins
1/4 cup butter, melted
2 cups whole milk
4 eggs, beaten
1/2 cup white sugar
1 teaspoon vanilla extract
1/2 teaspoon cinnamon powder

Directions:
1. In your slow cooker, combine the bread cubes, apples, pears, and raisins.
2. In a bowl, mix the butter, milk, eggs, sugar, vanilla, and cinnamon. Pour this mixture over the bread.
3. Cook for 5 hours on low heat with the lid on the pot.
4. Serve the bread pudding warm.

Creamy Coconut Tapioca Pudding

Time: 4 1/4 hours   **Servings: 6**

Ingredients:

1 cup water
1 teaspoon vanilla extract
1 cup tapioca pearls
1 cup coconut flakes
2 cups coconut milk
1/2 cup coconut sugar

Directions:

1. Mix all the ingredients in your slow cooker.
2. Cover and cook for 4 hours on low settings.
3. Serve the pudding warm or chilled.

Rich Chocolate Peanut Butter Cake

Time: 2 3/4 hours   **Servings: 8**

Ingredients:

1/2 teaspoon baking soda
3 eggs
3/4 cup sour cream
1/4 teaspoon salt
1 cup smooth peanut butter
1 1/2 cups all-purpose flour
1/4 cup cocoa powder
1 teaspoon baking powder
1/4 cup butter, softened
3/4 cup white sugar

Directions:

1. Mix the peanut butter, butter and sugar in a bowl until creamy.
2. Add the eggs, then pour in the flour, cocoa powder, baking powder, baking soda and salt.
3. Finally, add the sour cream and mix on high speed for 30 seconds.
4. Place the mixture in your slow cooker and cook for 2 1/4 hours on high settings.
5. Serve the cake cool.

One Bowl Chocolate Cake

Time: 4 1/4 hours   **Servings: 10**

Ingredients:

2 eggs
1 cup whole milk
1/2 cup canola oil
1 teaspoon baking powder
1 teaspoon vanilla extract
1/2 cup brewed coffee
1 teaspoon baking soda
1/2 teaspoon salt
1 1/2 cups sugar
1 1/2 cups all-purpose flour
1/2 cup cocoa powder

Directions:

1. Put all the necessary ingredients in a bowl and give it a quick mix.
2. Pour the mixture in the crock pot and cover.
3. Cook for 4 hours on low settings.
4. Allow it to cool in the pot before slicing and serving.

Oat Topped Apples

Time: 4 1/4 hours   **Servings: 6**

Ingredients:

2 tablespoons brown sugar
1 cup rolled oats
6 Granny Smith apples
1 cup golden raisins
1/2 cup apple cider
1/4 cup all-purpose flour
1/4 cup butter, chilled and cubed

Directions:

1. Core the apples and put them in your slow cooker.
2. Combine the raisins with brown sugar and stuff the apples with this mixture.
3. For the topping, mix the oats, flour and butter until grainy.
4. Pour the topping over each apple then pour the cider in the pot.
5. Cook for 4 hours on low settings.
6. Serve the apples cool.

Apple Cinnamon Brioche Pudding

Time: 6 1/2 hours   **Servings: 8**
Ingredients:
1 cup whole milk
4 eggs
1 teaspoon vanilla extract
1/2 teaspoon ground ginger
2 tablespoons white sugar
1 cup evaporated milk
16 oz. brioche bread, cubed
4 Granny Smith apples, peeled and cubed
1 teaspoon cinnamon powder
1 cup sweetened condensed milk

Directions:
1. Mix the brioche bread, apples, cinnamon, ginger, and sugar in your crock pot.
2. Combine the three types of milk in a bowl. Add the eggs and vanilla and mix well.
3. Pour this mix over the bread then cover the pot and cook for 6 hours on low settings.
4. The pudding is best served slightly warm.

Apple Cherry Cobbler

Time: 4 1/2 hours   **Servings: 10**
Ingredients:
1 pound cherries, pitted
4 red apples, peeled and sliced
4 tablespoons maple syrup
2 tablespoons cornstarch
1 tablespoon lemon juice
1 1/4 cups all-purpose flour
1/2 cup butter, chilled and cubed
2 tablespoons white sugar
1/2 cup buttermilk, chilled

Directions:
1. Mix the cherries, apples, maple syrup, cornstarch and lemon juice in your crock pot.
2. For the topping, combine the flour, butter and sugar in a bowl and mix well with your fingertips until grainy.
3. Add the buttermilk and mix.
4. Pour the mixture over the fruit mixture and bake for 4 hours on low settings.
5. Serve the cobbler cool.

Nutty Pear Streusel Dessert

Time: 4 1/2 hours   **Servings: 4**
Ingredients:
2 tablespoons melted butter
2 tablespoons brown sugar
1 pinch salt
1 teaspoon cinnamon powder
1/2 cup pecans, chopped
1 cup ground almonds
4 large apples, peeled and cubed
1/2 cup golden raisins
2 tablespoons all-purpose flour
4 pears
Directions:
1. Combine the apples, raisins, and cinnamon in your slow cooker.
2. For the topping, mix the pecans, almonds, flour, melted butter, sugar and salt.
3. Pour this mixture over the pears and cook on low settings for 4 hours.
4. Serve this dessert warm.

Pumpkin Croissant Pudding

Time: 5 1/4 hours   **Servings: 6**
Ingredients:
1 1/2 cups pumpkin puree
3 eggs
6 large croissants, cubed
1 teaspoon cinnamon powder
1/4 cup white sugar
1 cup skim milk

Directions:
1. Put the croissants in your crock pot.
2. Combine the milk, pumpkin puree, eggs, cinnamon and sugar in a bowl. Spread this mixture over the croissants.
3. Cover the pot and cook for 5 hours on low settings.
4. Serve the pudding cool.

Strawberry Fudgy Brownies

Time: 2 1/4 hours   **Servings: 8**
Ingredients:
2 eggs
1/2 cup white sugar
1/4 cup cocoa powder
1 pinch salt
1 1/2 cups fresh strawberries, halved
1/2 cup all-purpose flour
1/2 cup butter, cubed
1 cup dark chocolate chips
1/2 cup applesauce

Directions:
1. Add the butter and chocolate in a bowl and place over a hot water bath to melt.
2. Remove from heat and add the eggs, sugar and applesauce and mix.
3. Add the cocoa powder, flour and salt and pour the mixture in your slow cooker.
4. Top with strawberries and cook for 2 hours on high settings.
5. Allow to cool before cutting into cubes and serving.

Caramel Pear Pudding Cake

Time: 4 1/2 hours   **Servings: 6**
Ingredients:
1/2 cup sugar
1/4 teaspoon salt
1/2 teaspoon cinnamon powder
4 ripe pears, cored and sliced
3/4 cup caramel sauce
2/3 cup all-purpose flour
1 teaspoon baking powder
1/4 cup butter, melted
1/4 cup whole milk

Directions:
1. Add the sugar, flour, baking powder, salt, and cinnamon in a bowl. Add the butter and milk and give it a fast mix.
2. Put the pears in your crock pot and top with the mixture.
3. Drizzle the mixture with caramel sauce and cook for 4 hours on low settings.
4. Allow the cake to cool before serving.

Walnut Apple Crisp

Time: 4 1/2 hours   **Servings: 6**
Ingredients:
4 tablespoons light brown sugar
1 pinch salt
1/4 cup butter, melted
Caramel sauce for serving
1 tablespoon lemon juice
1/2 cup all-purpose flour
1 cup ground walnuts
2 tablespoons white sugar
1 tablespoon cornstarch
1 1/2 pounds Granny Smith apples, peeled, cored and sliced
1 teaspoon cinnamon powder
1 teaspoon ground ginger

Directions:
1. Combine the ginger, light brown sugar, apples, cinnamon, lemon juice and cornstarch in a slow cooker.
2. For the topping, combine the flour, walnuts, white sugar, salt and butter in a bowl.
3. Spread this mixture over the apples and cover.
4. Cook for 4 hours on low settings.
5. Serve the crisp cool with caramel sauce.

Lemon Berry Cake

Time: 4 1/2 hours   **Servings: 10**
Ingredients:
2 teaspoons lemon zest
4 eggs
1 cup butter, softened
1 teaspoon baking powder
1/4 teaspoon salt
1 cup fresh mixed berries
1 cup white sugar
1 teaspoon vanilla extract
1 cup all-purpose flour

Directions:
1. Combine the butter, sugar and vanilla in a bowl until creamy.
2. Add the eggs and lemon zest and mix for 1 minute on high speed.
3. Combine the baking powder, flour, berries, and salt then add the mixture in your slow cooker.
4. Cover and cook the mixture for 4 hours on low settings.
5. Allow it to cool before serving.

Silky Chocolate Fondue

Time: 2 1/4 hours   **Servings: 6**
Ingredients:
2 tablespoons dark rum
1/4 cup whole milk
1 1/2 cups dark chocolate chips
1 cup heavy cream
1/4 cup sweetened condensed milk
Fresh fruits of your choice for serving
(strawberries, grapes, bananas, kiwi fruits)

Directions:
1. Mix the cream, two types of milk, chocolate chips and rum in your slow cooker.
2. Cover and cook the mixture for 2 hours on low settings.
3. Serve the fondue by add fresh fruits into it.

Orange Ginger Cheesecake

Time: 7 1/2 hours   **Servings: 8**
Ingredients:
Crust:
1 tablespoon grated orange zest
6 oz. graham crackers, crushed
1/2 cup butter, melted
Filling:
1 pinch salt
1 tablespoon cornstarch
1 teaspoon grated ginger
20 oz. cream cheese
1 cup sour cream
4 eggs
1 teaspoon grated orange zest
1/2 cup white sugar

Directions:
1. For the crust, combine the two ingredients together in a bowl then transfer in your crock pot and press the mixture well on the bottom of the pot.
2. For the filling, mix all the necessary ingredients in a bowl then pour the mix over the crust.
3. Cover the pot and cook for 7 hours on low settings.
4. Allow the cheesecake to cool before slicing and serving.

White Chocolate Apricot Bread Pudding

Time: 5 1/2 hours   **Servings: 8**
Ingredients:
1 cup white chocolate chips
2 cups milk
8 cups one day old bread cubes
1 cup dried apricots, diced
1 teaspoon vanilla extract
1 teaspoon orange zest
1 cup heavy cream
4 eggs
1/2 cup white sugar

Directions:
1. Combine the bread, apricots and chocolate chips in your slow cooker.
2. Put the milk, cream, eggs, vanilla, orange zest and sugar in a bowl and mix.
3. Pour this mixture over the bread pudding then cover the pot and cook for 5 hours on low settings.
4. The pudding is best served slightly warm.

Coconut Poached Pears

Time: 6 1/4 hours   **Servings: 6**
Ingredients:
6 ripe but firm pears
2 cups coconut milk
2 cups water
1 cinnamon stick
1 star anise
3/4 cup coconut sugar
2 lemon rings

Directions:
1. Peel and place the pears in your slow cooker.
2. Add the remaining ingredients and cover. Cook for 6 hours on low settings.
3. Allow the pears to cool in the pot before serving.

Chocolate Walnut Bread

Time: 2 1/2 hours   **Servings: 8**

Ingredients:

1/2 cup canola oil
1 teaspoon vanilla extract
1 cup whole milk
3 eggs
1/4 cup sour cream
1/2 cup light brown sugar
1/4 teaspoon salt
1 teaspoon baking powder
1 cup all-purpose flour
1/2 cup cocoa powder
1 cup walnuts, chopped

Directions:

1. Mix the milk, eggs, canola oil, vanilla, sugar and sour cream in a bowl.
2. Add the remaining ingredients and stir quickly just until combined.
3. Pour the mixture in your crock pot and cook on high settings for 2 hours.
4. Allow it to cool in the pot before serving.

Egyptian Rice Pudding

Time: 4 1/4 hours   **Servings: 6**

Ingredients:

1 vanilla pod, cut in half lengthwise
1/4 cup cold water
1/2 cup sugar
2 tablespoons cornstarch
1 1/2 cups white rice
4 cups whole milk
1 teaspoon cinnamon powder

Directions:

1. Combine the rice, milk, vanilla pod and sugar in your crock pot.
2. Cook for 3 hours on low settings.
3. Mix the water and cornstarch in a bowl then pour this mixture over the rice pudding.
4. Cover and cook for 1 additional hour on low settings.
5. Serve the pudding warm or cook and sprinkle with cinnamon powder.

Ginger Fruit Compote

Time: 6 1/2 hours   **Servings: 6**

Ingredients:

2 whole cloves
1/2 cup dried apricots, halved
2 ripe pears, peeled and cubed
2 red apples, peeled, cored and sliced
4 slices fresh pineapple, cubed
2 cups water
1 star anise
1 cup fresh orange juice
3 tablespoons light brown sugar
1 cinnamon stick

Directions:

1. Place all the necessary ingredients in your slow cooker.
2. Cover and cook the mixture for 6 hours on low settings.
3. Allow to cool before serving.

Molten Chocolate Cake

Time: 2 1/2 hours   **Servings: 6**

Ingredients:

1/4 cup cocoa powder
1 teaspoon baking powder
1 teaspoon vanilla extract
1 cup sugar
4 eggs
1/2 cup butter, melted
1 cup all-purpose flour
1/4 teaspoon salt

Directions:

1. Combine the eggs, butter, vanilla and sugar in a bowl until creamy.
2. Add the cocoa powder, flour, and salt and mix, but don't over-mix the mixture.
3. Pour the mixture in your crock pot and cook for 2 hours on high settings.
4. Serve the cake warm.

Amarena Cherry Cola Cake

Time: 4 1/4 hours   **Servings: 8**
Ingredients:
1/2 cup butter, melted
1 teaspoon vanilla extract
1 cup cola
1/2 teaspoon baking powder
1/2 teaspoon baking soda
1/4 cup light brown sugar
1/4 cup cocoa powder
1/2 cup whole milk
1 1/2 cups all-purpose flour
1/4 teaspoon salt
2 cups Amarena cherries, pitted

Directions:
1. Combine the cola, sugar, butter, vanilla and milk in a bowl.
2. Add the cocoa powder, flour, salt, baking powder and baking soda and give it a fast mix.
3. Add the cherries. Pour the mixture into the empty slow cooker and cook on low settings for 4 hours.
4. Allow the cake to cool before slicing and serving.

Crock Pot Crème Brulee

Time: 6 1/4 hours   **Servings: 4**
Ingredients:
2 egg yolks
2 whole eggs
2 1/2 cups milk
1 1/2 cups heavy cream
2 tablespoons white sugar
1 teaspoon vanilla extract
2 tablespoons maple syrup
1 cup sugar for topping
Directions:
1. Combine the egg yolks, eggs, milk, cream, vanilla, maple syrup and white sugar in a bowl.
2. Pour the mixture in 4 ramekins and place the ramekins in your slow cooker.
3. Add water into the slow cooker, which will be enough to cover ¾ of the ramekins.
4. Cover the pot and cook for 6 hours on low settings.
5. When done, pour the remaining sugar over the crème brulee and caramelize it using a blow torch.

No Crust Lemon Cheesecake

Time: 6 1/4 hours   **Servings: 8**
Ingredients:
4 eggs
2 tablespoons cornstarch
24 oz. cream cheese
2/3 cup white sugar
1 teaspoon vanilla extract
1/2 cup heavy cream
1 lemon, zested and juiced

Directions:
1. Put all the necessary ingredients in a bowl and mix well.
2. Pour the mixture in your greased slow cooker and cook on low settings for 6 hours.
3. Serve the cheesecake cool.

Fudgy Peanut Butter Cake

Time: 2 1/4 hours   **Servings: 8**
Ingredients:
3/4 cup white sugar
1 teaspoon vanilla extract
1/2 cup smooth peanut butter
1/4 cup canola oil
1/4 cup cocoa powder
1 teaspoon baking powder
2 eggs
1/4 cup whole milk
1 cup all-purpose flour
1/4 teaspoon salt

Directions:
1. Combine the peanut butter, canola oil, sugar, vanilla and eggs in a bowl and mix until smooth and creamy.
2. Add the milk as well as the flour, cocoa powder, baking powder, and salt.
3. Place the mixture in your slow cooker and cook on high settings for 2 hours.
4. Allow it to cool in the pot before slicing and serving.

Spiced Rice Pudding

Time: 4 1/4 hours   **Servings: 6**
Ingredients:
3 cups whole milk
1 star anise
1/2-inch piece of ginger, sliced
1/2 teaspoon rose water
2 whole cloves
1 cinnamon stick
1 cup Arborio rice
1/2 cup white sugar

Directions:
1. Put all the necessary ingredients in your slow cooker.
2. Cover and cook for 4 hours on low settings.
3. Serve either warm or cool.

Spiced Poached Pears

Time: 6 1/2 hours   **Servings: 6**
Ingredients;
3/4 cup white sugar
1 star anise
6 ripe but firm pears
2 cups white wine
2 cinnamon stick
1 1/2 cups water
1-inch piece of ginger, sliced
4 whole cloves
2 cardamom pods, crushed

Directions:
1. Peel and place the pears in your slow cooker.
2. Add the remaining ingredients and cook for 6 hours on low settings.
3. Serve the pears cool.

Tiramisu Bread Pudding

Time: 4 1/4 hours   **Servings: 6**
Ingredients:
2 eggs
2 tablespoons cocoa powder
2 tablespoons Kahlua
1/2 cup mascarpone cheese
6 cups bread cubes
1/4 cup white sugar
2 teaspoons coffee powder
1 1/2 cups milk

Directions:
1. Mix the sugar, coffee, Kahlua, mascarpone cheese, milk and eggs in a bowl.
2. Place the bread cubes in a slow cooker then pour the milk mixture over the bread.
3. Sprinkle with cocoa powder and cook on low settings for 4 hours.
4. Serve the pudding slightly warm.

Amaretti Cheesecake

Time: 6 1/2 hours   **Servings: 8**
Ingredients:
Crust:
1/4 cup butter, melted
6 oz. Amaretti cookies, crushed
Filling:
24 oz. cream cheese
1/2 cup sour cream
4 eggs
1/2 cup white sugar
1 tablespoon vanilla extract
1 tablespoon Amaretto liqueur

Directions:
1. Combine the crushed cookies with butter then place the mixture in your crockpot.
2. For the filling, combine the sugar, vanilla, cream cheese, sour cream, eggs, and liqueur and give it a fast mix.
3. Pour the filling mixture over the crust and cook for 6 hours on low settings.
4. Let the cheesecake to cool before slicing and serving.

Brandied Brioche Pudding

Time: 6 1/2 hours   **Servings: 8**
Ingredients:
2 cups whole milk
1/4 cup brandy
10 oz. brioche bread, cubed
4 eggs, beaten
1 teaspoon vanilla extract
1/2 cup light brown sugar

Directions:
1. Place the brioche in a slow cooker.
2. Mix the eggs, milk, brandy, sugar and vanilla in a bowl then pour this mixture over the brioche.
3. Cover and cook on low settings for 6 hours.
4. Serve the pudding slightly warm.

Pineapple Coconut Tapioca Pudding

Time: 6 1/4 hours   **Servings: 8**
Ingredients:
1 cup sweetened condensed milk
1 teaspoon vanilla extract
1 can crushed pineapple
1 1/2 cups tapioca pearls
2 cups coconut milk
1/2 cup coconut flakes

Directions:
1. Put all the necessary ingredients in your crock pot.
2. Cover and cook on low settings for 6 hours.
3. Serve the pudding warm.

Vanilla Bean Caramel Custard

Time: 6 1/4 hours   **Servings: 6**
Ingredients:
1 cup heavy cream
2 egg yolks
1 tablespoon vanilla bean paste
2 tablespoons white sugar
1 cup white sugar for melting
4 cups whole milk
4 eggs

Directions:
1. Caramelize 1 cup of sugar in a pan until it has an amber color. Pour the caramel in a slow cooker.
2. Combine the milk, cream, egg yolks, eggs, vanilla bean paste and sugar in a bowl. Pour this mixture over the caramel.
3. Cover and cook on low settings for 6 hours.
4. Serve the custard cool.

Cardamom Coconut Rice Pudding

Time: 6 1/4 hours   **Servings: 6**
Ingredients:
1 cup coconut water
Sliced peaches for serving
1/2 cup coconut sugar
1 1/4 cups Arborio rice
2 cups coconut milk
4 cardamom pods, crushed

Directions:
1. Put all the necessary ingredients in your crock pot.
2. Cover and cook on low settings for 6 hours.
3. Serve the pudding warm or cool. For more flavor, top the pudding with sliced peaches just before serving.

Rocky Road Chocolate Cake

Time: 4 1/2 hours   **Servings: 10**

Ingredients:

1 1/2 cups all-purpose flour
1/2 cup cocoa powder
1 teaspoon baking soda
1/2 teaspoon salt
1/2 cup canola oil
1 cup buttermilk
1/2 cup whole milk
1 teaspoon vanilla extract
2 eggs
1/2 cup mini marshmallows
1/2 cup pecans, chopped
1/2 cup white chocolate chips

Directions:

1. Combine the cocoa powder, flour, baking soda, salt, canola oil, buttermilk, milk, vanilla and eggs in a bowl. Place the mixture in your slow cooker.
2. Top the mixture with mini marshmallows, pecans and chocolate chips.
3. Cover and cook on low settings for 4 hours.
4. Allow the cake to cool completely before serving.

Ricotta Lemon Cake

Time: 5 1/4 hours   **Servings: 8**

Ingredients:

1 1/2 cups ricotta cheese
1/4 cup butter, melted
1/2 cup white sugar
1 teaspoon vanilla extract
1 tablespoon lemon zest
4 eggs, separated
1 1/2 cups all-purpose flour
1 1/2 teaspoons baking powder
1/4 teaspoon salt

Directions:

1. Grease your slow cooker with butter.
2. Combine the sugar, egg yolks, ricotta, butter, vanilla, and lemon zest in a bowl. Add the flour, baking powder, and salt.
3. Whip the egg whites, then add into the mixtures.
4. Pour the mixture in a crock pot and cook for 5 hours on low settings.
5. Allow the cake to cool before slicing and serving.

Sour Cream Cheesecake

Time: 4 1/4 hours   **Servings: 8**

Ingredients:

Crust:
1/2 cup butter, melted
1 1/2 cups crushed graham crackers
Filling:
4 eggs
1/2 cup white sugar
12 oz. sour cream
1 tablespoon cornstarch
12 oz. cream cheese
1 tablespoon vanilla extract
1/2 teaspoon almond extract

Directions:

1. For the crust, combine the graham crackers with the butter in a bowl then place this mixture in a slow cooker.
2. For the filling, put the cream cheese, cornstarch, vanilla, sour cream, eggs, sugar, and almond extract in a bowl. Pour the mixture over the crust.
3. Cook on low settings for 4 hours.
4. Allow the cheesecake to cool before slicing and serving.

Maple Roasted Pears

Time: 6 1/4 hours   **Servings: 4**

Ingredients:

1 teaspoon grated ginger
1 cinnamon stick
1/4 cup white wine
1/2 cup water
1/4 cup maple syrup
2 cardamom pods, crushed
4 ripe pears, carefully peeled and cored

Directions:

1. Put all the necessary ingredients in your slow cooker.
2. Cover and cook on low settings for 6 hours.
3. Allow to cool before serving.

Apple Granola Crumble

Time: 6 1/4 hours   **Servings: 4**
Ingredients:
2 tablespoons honey
1 1/2 cups granola
4 red apples, peeled, cored and sliced
1/2 teaspoon cinnamon powder

Directions:
1. Mix the apples and honey in your crock pot.
2. Top with the granola and sprinkle with cinnamon.
3. Cover and cook on low settings for 6 hours.
4. Serve the crumble warm.

Mixed Nuts Brownies

Time: 4 1/4 hours   **Servings: 12**
Ingredients:
1 cup white sugar
3 eggs
8 oz. dark chocolate, chopped
1/2 cup butter
1/2 cup cocoa powder
1/2 teaspoon salt
1 teaspoon vanilla extract
1 cup all-purpose flour
1 cup mixed nuts, chopped

Directions:
1. Add the chocolate and butter into a bowl and place over a hot water bath.
2. Take from heat and add the flour, cocoa powder, eggs, sugar, vanilla, and salt and mix gently.
3. Add the nuts then place the mixture in your slow cooker.
4. Cover and cook the mixture for 4 hours on low settings.
5. Allow to cool before cutting into small squares.

Peanut Butter Chocolate Chips Bars

Time: 2 1/4 hours   **Servings: 12**
Ingredients:
2 eggs
1 cup light brown sugar
1 cup dark chocolate chips
1 cup pecans, chopped
1 cup all-purpose flour
1/2 cup butter, melted
1/2 cup smooth peanut butter
1/4 teaspoon salt

Directions:
1. Mix the butter, peanut butter, eggs and brown sugar in a bowl until creamy and smooth.
2. Add the flour and salt then place the mixture in a slow cooker
3. Add chocolate chips and pecans and cook on for 2 hours high settings.
4. Allow to cool before slicing and serving.

Golden Raisin Brioche Pudding

Time: 2 1/2 hours   **Servings: 6**
Ingredients:
2 tablespoons brandy
1/4 cup white sugar
4 eggs
6 cups brioche cubes
1 cup golden raisins
2 cups whole milk

Directions:
1. Combine the brioche cubes and raisins in a slow cooker.
2. Mix the milk, brandy, eggs, and sugar in a bowl then pour this mixture over the brioche.
3. Cover and cook on high settings for 2 hours.
4. Serve the pudding warm.

Coconut Condensed Milk Custard

Time: 5 1/4 hours   **Servings: 6**
Ingredients:
1 1/4 cups sweetened condensed milk
1 tablespoon vanilla extract
6 eggs
1 cup evaporated milk
1 can (15 oz.) coconut milk
1 teaspoon lime zest

Directions:
1. Combine the eggs, coconut milk, condensed milk, vanilla, lime zest and evaporated milk in a bowl.
2. Place the mixture in the slow cooker.
3. Cover and cook on low settings for 5 hours.
4. Allow to cool before serving.

Peppermint Chocolate Clusters

Time: 4 1/4 hours   **Servings: 20**
Ingredients:
1/2 cup milk chocolate chips
1 teaspoon peppermint extract
2 cups pretzels, chopped
1 1/2 cups dark chocolate chips
1 cup pecans, chopped

Directions:
1. Mix all the ingredients in your slow cooker.
2. Cover and cook on low settings for 4 hours.
3. When done, drop small clusters of mixture on a baking tray lined with baking paper.
4. Allow to cool then serve.

Buttery Chocolate Cake

Time: 4 1/4 hours   **Servings: 10**
Ingredients:
4 eggs
1 cup dark chocolate, melted and chilled
1/2 cup sour cream
3/4 cup butter, softened
3/4 cup light brown sugar
1 1/2 teaspoons baking powder
1/4 teaspoon salt
1 1/4 cups all-purpose flour
1/4 cup cocoa powder

Directions:
1. Stir the butter and sugar in a bowl until creamy. Add the eggs then stir in the melted chocolate and sour cream.
2. Add the flour, cocoa powder, baking powder, and salt.
3. Place the mixture in your slow cooker and cook on low settings for 4 hours.
4. Allow the cake to cool before serving.

S'Mores Fondue

Time: 1 1/4 hours   **Servings: 6**
Ingredients:
1/2 teaspoon all-spice powder
1 1/2 cups dark chocolate chips
1 cup mini marshmallows
1/2 cup caramel sauce
1/2 cup heavy cream
1 can (15 oz.) sweetened condensed milk
Pretzels or fresh fruits for serving

Directions:
1. Combine the milk, caramel sauce, cream, chocolate chips, all-spice powder, and marshmallows in your slow cooker.
2. Cover and cook for 1 hour on high settings.
3. Serve the fondue warm with pretzels of fresh fruits.

Double Chocolate Cake

Time: 4 1/4 hours   **Servings: 8**
Ingredients:
1/4 teaspoon salt
1/4 cup cocoa powder
1 1/2 cups all-purpose flour
1 1/2 teaspoons baking powder
1 cup dark chocolate chips
4 eggs
1 teaspoon vanilla extract
1/2 cup vegetable oil
1 cup water
1 cup sour cream

Directions:
1. Combine the flour, baking powder, salt, cocoa powder in a bowl.
2. Add the water, oil, sour cream, eggs, vanilla extract and mix quickly.
3. Place the mixture in your slow cooker and top with chocolate chips.
4. Cover and cook on low settings for 4 hours.
5. Allow to cool before serving.

Saucy Apple and Pears

Time: 6 1/4 hours   **Servings: 6**
Ingredients:
1/4 cup light brown sugar
1 cup water
1 cinnamon stick
1/4 cup butter
1 cup apple juice
1 star anise
4 ripe pears, peeled, cored and sliced
2 Granny Smith apples, peeled, cored and sliced

Directions:
1. Mix all the ingredients in the crock pot.
2. Cover and cook on low settings for 6 hours.
3. Allow to cool in the pot before serving.

Blueberry Dumpling Pie

Time: 5 1/2 hours   **Servings: 8**
Ingredients:
1/4 cup light brown sugar
1 tablespoon lemon zest
1/2 cup butter, chilled and cubed
1 1/2 cups all-purpose flour
2 tablespoons white sugar
2/3 cup buttermilk, chilled
1 1/2 pounds fresh blueberries
2 tablespoons cornstarch
1/2 teaspoon salt
1 teaspoon baking powder
Directions:
1. Combine the cornstarch, blueberries, brown sugar and lemon zest in your slow cooker.
2. For the dumpling topping, put the flour, salt, sugar, baking powder, and butter in a bowl and mix until sandy.
3. Add the buttermilk and mix quickly.
4. Pour the mixture over the blueberries and cook on low settings for 5 hours.
5. Allow to cool completely before serving.

Dried Fruit Rice Pudding

Time: 6 1/4 hours   **Servings: 8**
Ingredients:
1/2 cup dried apricots, chopped
1/4 cup dried cranberries
1/2 cup white sugar
3 cups whole milk
2 cups white rice
1/2 cup golden raisins
1 1/4 cups heavy cream
1 cinnamon stick

Directions:
1. Combine the rice, milk, cream, raisins, apricots, cranberries, sugar, and cinnamon in your crock pot.
2. Cover and cook on low settings for 6 hours.
3. Serve the rice pudding warm.

CHAPTER 6

BEANS AND GRAINS RECIPES

Apple Bean Pot

Time: 3½ to 4½ hours   **Serves: 12**
Ingredients
3 tart apples, peeled and chopped
½ cup ketchup or barbecue sauce
1 (53-ounce / 1.5-kg) can baked beans, well drained
1 large onion, chopped
½ cup firmly packed brown sugar
Hot dogs, or chopped ham chunks (optional)
1 package smoky cocktail sausages, or chopped

Directions

1. Put beans in crock pot.

2. Add onions and apples then mix well.

3. Add ketchup or barbecue sauce, brown sugar, ham, and sausages then mix.

4. Cover and heat on low settings for 3 to 4 hours, and then on high settings 30 minutes.

Chili Boston Baked Beans

Time: 6 to 8 hours   **Serves: 20**
Ingredients
2 tart apples, diced
1 cup chili sauce
1 cup raisins
2 small onions, diced
3 teaspoons dry mustard
½ cup sweet pickle relish
1 cup chopped ham or crumbled bacon
2 (15-ounce / 425-g) cans baked beans

Directions

1. Combine together all the ingredients.

2. Cover and cook on low settings for 6 to 8 hours. Serve

Never Fail Rice

Time: 2 to 6 hours   **Serves: 6**
Ingredients
2 cups water
½ tablespoon butter
½ teaspoon salt
1 cup long-grain rice, uncooked

Directions

1. Put all the ingredients in small crock pot.

2. Cover and cook on low settings for 4 to 6 hours, or on high settings for 2 to 3 hours, or until rice is just fully cooked.

3. Serve.

Herb Rice

Time: 4 to 6 hours   **Serves: 6**
Ingredients
 1 teaspoon dried rosemary
½ teaspoon dried marjoram
1 tablespoon butter or margarine
3 chicken bouillon cubes
3 cups water
1½ cups long-grain rice, uncooked
¼ cup onions, diced
¼ cup dried parsley, chopped
½ cup slivered almonds (optional)

Directions

1. Combine the chicken bouillon cubes and water.

2. Mix all the ingredients in crock pot.

3. Cook on low settings for 4 to 6 hours, or until rice is fully cooked.

Wild Rice

Time: 2½ to 3 hours   **Serves: 5**

Ingredients

1 tablespoon oil
½ teaspoon salt
½ cup sliced fresh mushrooms
½ cup diced onions
½ cup diced green or red bell peppers
¼ teaspoon black pepper
1 cup wild rice, uncooked
2½ cups fat-free, low-sodium chicken broth

Directions

1. Put the rice and vegetables in crock pot. Pour oil, salt, and pepper over vegetables and mix.

2. Heat the chicken broth. Pour over all the ingredients in crock pot.

3. Cover and cook on high settings for 2½ to 3 hours, or until rice is soft and liquid is absorbed. Serve.

Risi Bisi (Peas and Rice)

Time: 2½ to 3½ hours   **Serves: 6**

Ingredients

2 garlic cloves, minced
2 (14½-ounce / 411-g) cans reduced-sodium chicken broth
⅓ cup water
¾ teaspoon Italian seasoning
½ cup frozen baby peas, thawed
¼ cup grated Parmesan cheese
1½ cups converted long-grain white rice, uncooked
¾ cup chopped onions
½ teaspoon dried basil leaves

Directions

1. Put the rice, onions, and garlic in crock pot.

2. In saucepan, combine the chicken broth and water then boil. Add Italian seasoning and basil leaves.

3. Stir into rice mixture.

4. Cover and cook on low settings for 2 to 3 hours, or until liquid is absorbed.

5. Add peas then Cover and cook for 30 minutes. Add cheese. Serve.

Hometown Spanish Rice

Time: 2 to 4 hours   **Serves: 6 to 8**

Ingredients

1 large onion, chopped
1 bell pepper, chopped
2 cups long-grain rice, cooked
Grated Parmesan cheese (optional)
1 (28-ounce / 794-g) can stewed tomatoes with juice
Nonstick cooking spray
1 pound (454 g) bacon, cooked, and broken into bite-size pieces

Directions

1. Heat the onion and pepper in a small nonstick frying pan until soft.

2. Spray interior of the crock pot with nonstick cooking spray.

3. Put all ingredients in the crock pot.

4. Cover and cook on low settings for 4 hours, or on high settings for 2 hours, or until heated through.

5. Add Parmesan cheese before serving (Optional).

Rice 'n Beans 'n Salsa

Time: 4 to 10 hours   **Serves: 6 to 8**

Ingredients

1 (14-ounce / 397-g) chicken broth
1 quart salsa, your choice of heat
1 cup water
½ teaspoon garlic powder
1 cup long-grain white or brown rice, uncooked
2 (16-ounce / 454-g) cans black or navy beans, drained

Directions

1. Put all the ingredients in crock pot. Mix well.

2. Cover and cook on low settings for 8 to 10 hours, or on high settings for 4 hours.

Red Bean and Brown Rice Stew

Time: 6 hours   **Serves: 6**
Ingredients
¾ cup brown rice, uncooked
4 cups water
2 cups dried red beans
1 large onion, cut into chunks
1 tablespoon cumin
6 carrots.

Directions

1. Put the dried beans in crock pot and cover with water. Allow to soak for 8 hours or overnight then drain.

2. Return soaked beans to cooker. Add all the remaining ingredients.

3. Cover and cook on low settings for 6 hours.

Broccoli-Rice Casserole

Time: 3 to 4 hours   **Serves: 6**
Ingredients
1 cup minute rice, uncooked
1 (8-ounce / 227-g) jar processed cheese spread
1 (1-pound / 454-g) package frozen chopped broccoli
1 (10¾-ounce / 305-g) can cream of mushroom soup

Directions

1. Combine all the ingredients in crock pot.

2. Cover and cook on high settings for 3 to 4 hours, or until rice and broccoli are soft but not mushy or dry.

Wild Rice Pilaf

Time: 3½ to 5 hours   **Serves: 6**
Ingredients
2 cups water
1 (14-ounce / 397-g) chicken broth
1½ cups wild rice, uncooked
½ cup finely chopped onion
½ teaspoon dried thyme leaves
Nonstick cooking spray
1 (4-ounce / 113-g) can sliced mushrooms, drained

Directions

1. Spray crock pot with nonstick cooking spray.

2. Wash the rice and drain well then put rice, onion, chicken broth, and water in crock pot. Mix properly.

3. Cover and cook on high settings for 3 to 4 hours.

4. Add mushrooms and thyme and mix gently.

5. Cover and cook on low settings for 30 to 60 minutes longer, or until wild rice is soft.

Flavorful Fruited Rice

Time: 2 hours   **Serves: 4**
Ingredients
¼ cup chopped dried apricots
Nonstick cooking spray
2 cups chicken broth
¼ cup dried cranberries
⅓ cup chopped onion
1 (6-ounce / 170-g) package long-grain and wild rice mixture
Directions

1. Spray small frying pan with nonstick cooking spray.

2. Add chopped onions and cook on medium heat about 5 minutes.

3. Put onions and the remaining ingredients in the crock pot, as well as the seasonings. Mix well to dissolve seasonings.

4. Cover and cook on high settings for 2 hours.

5. Serve.

Cheddar Rice

Time: 2 to 3 hours   Serves: 8 to 10

Ingredients

½ teaspoon pepper
1 teaspoon salt
5 cups water
2 cups shredded Cheddar cheese
1 cup slivered almonds (optional)
2 cups brown rice, uncooked
3 tablespoons butter
½ cup thinly sliced green onions or shallots

Directions

1. Put rice, butter, green onion, and salt in crock pot.

2. Boil the water and pour over rice mixture.

3. Cover and cook on high settings for 2 to 3 hours, or until rice is tender and liquid is absorbed.

4. Five minutes before serving stir in pepper and cheese.

5. Garnish with slivered almonds, if you wish.

Makes-A-Meal Baked Beans

Time: 3 hours   Serves: 6 to 8

Ingredients

1 pound (454 g) ground beef
½ cup chopped onions
½ teaspoon taco seasoning, or more
1 or 2 (15-ounce / 425-g) cans pork and beans
¾ cup barbecue sauce

Directions

1. Heat the ground beef and onions in a nonstick pan. Drain.

2. Combine all the ingredients in the crock pot, including the browned ground beef and onions.

3. Cover and cook on low setting for 3 hours.

4. Serve.

Refried Beans with Bacon

Time: 5 hours   Serves: 8

Ingredients

2 garlic cloves, minced
2 cups dried red or pinto beans
6 cups water
1 teaspoon salt
½ pound (227 g) bacon
Shredded cheese
1 large tomato or 1 pint tomato juice

Directions

1. Put the beans, water, garlic, tomato, and salt in crock pot.

2. Cover and cook on high settings for 5 hours, stirring occasionally. When the beans become tender, drain off some water.

3. Put the bacon in a pan. Drain and crumble the bacon. Add half of bacon and 3 tablespoons drippings to beans then mix.

4. Blend the beans with a blender. Fry the bean mixture in the remaining bacon drippings. Add more salt.

5. Sprinkle the rest of the bacon and shredded cheese on top of beans.

No-Meat Baked Beans

Time: 6½ to 9½ hours   Serves: 8 to 10

Ingredients

1 small onion, chopped	¾ cup ketchup
½ cup brown sugar	¾ cup water
1 teaspoon dry mustard	6 cups water
3 tablespoons dark molasses	1 teaspoon salt
1 pound (454 g) dried navy beans	

Directions

1. Soak beans in water overnight. Cook beans in water until tender, about 1½ hours. Drain, discarding bean water.

2. Add all ingredients in the crock pot. Mix well.

3. Cover and cook on low settings for 5 to 8 hours, or until beans are well flavored.

Bean Serve

Time: 6 to 8 hours   **Serves: 12**

Ingredients

1 tablespoon garlic powder
1 tablespoon parsley flakes
1 tablespoon dried oregano
2 cups diced carrots
2 (15-ounce / 425-g) cans diced tomatoes
1 tablespoon ground cumin
2 (15-ounce / 425-g) cans kidney beans, drained and rinsed
2 (15-ounce / 425-g) cans pinto beans, drained and rinsed.

2 cups water
1 cup minced onions
2 cups diced celery
1 tablespoon salt

Directions

1. Place turkey with onions in a nonstick skillet over medium heat. Add celery and carrots and cook. Place in crock pot.

2. Add the remaining ingredients. Stir to mix properly.

3. Cover and cook on low settings for 6 to 8 hours.

4. Serve.

Pizza Rice

Time: 6 to 10 hours   **Serves: 6**

Ingredients

2½ cups water
2 cups rice, uncooked
3 cups chunky pizza sauce
4 ounces (113 g) pepperoni, sliced
1 cup shredded cheese
1 (7-ounce / 170-g) can mushrooms, undrained.

Directions

1. Mix rice, sauce, water, mushrooms, and pepperoni.

2. Cover and cook on low settings for 10 hours, or on high settings for 6 hours.

3. Sprinkle with cheese before serving.

Easy Wheat Berries

Time: 2 hours   **Serves: 4 to 6**

Ingredients

½ cup dried raisins
1 (14½-ounce / 411-g) can broth
½ to 1 broth can of water
1 cup wheat berries
1 cup couscous or small pasta like orzo

Directions

1. Cover wheat berries with water and soak for 2 hours before cooking. Place wheat berries into the crock pot.

2. Mix with the remaining ingredients in the crock pot.

3. Cover and cook on low settings until liquid is absorbed and berries are soft, about 2 hours.

Arroz con Queso

Time: 6 to 9 hours   **Serves: 6 to 8**

Ingredients

1 tablespoon oil
3 garlic cloves, minced
1½ cups long-grain rice, uncooked
1 cup shredded Monterey Jack cheese
1 teaspoon salt
1 cup shredded Monterey Jack cheese
1 large onion, finely chopped
1 cup cottage cheese
1 (4¼-ounce / 120-g) can chopped green chili peppers, drained
1 (14½-ounce / 411-g) can whole tomatoes, mashed
1 (15-ounce / 425-g) can Mexican style beans, undrained

Directions

1. Mix all the ingredients except final cup of cheese. Pour into well-greased crock pot.

2. Cover and cook on low settings for 6 to 9 hours.

3. Sprinkle with the remaining cheese before serving.

Barbecued Lentils

Time: 6 to 8 hours   **Serves: 8**
Ingredients
2 cups barbecue sauce
3½ cups water
1 pound (454 g) dry lentils
1 package vegetarian hot dogs, sliced

Directions
1. Mix all the ingredients in crock pot.

2. Cover and cook on low settings for 6 to 8 hours.

3. Serve

Bacon and Beef Calico Beans

Time: 2 to 6 hours   **Serves: 10**
Ingredients
¼ to ½ pound (227 g) bacon
1 pound (454 g) ground beef
1 medium onion, chopped
1 (2-pound / 907-g) can pork and beans
1 (1-pound / 454-g) can Great Northern beans, drained
1 (14½-ounce / 411-g) can French-style green beans, drained
½ cup brown sugar
½ cup ketchup
½ teaspoon salt
2 tablespoons cider vinegar
1 tablespoon prepared mustard

Directions
1. Heat the bacon, ground beef, and onion in a pan until soft then drain.

2. Mix all the ingredients in crock pot.

3. Cover and cook on low settings for 5 to 6 hours, or on high settings for 2 to 3 hours.

4. Serve.

Smoky Beans

Time: 4 to 6 hours   **Serves: 10 to 12**
Ingredients
1 tablespoon prepared mustard
2 tablespoons brown sugar
1 (16-ounce / 454-g) can kidney beans, drained
1 cup ketchup
1 teaspoon salt
1 large onion, chopped
1 pound (454 g) ground beef, browned
1 (15-ounce / 425-g) can pork and beans
2 tablespoons hickory-flavored barbecue sauce
1 (15-ounce / 425-g) can ranch-style beans, drained
½ to 1 pound (227 to 454 g) small smoky link sausages (optional)
Directions
1. Heat the ground beef and onion in a pan. Place into crock pot and set on high setting.

2. Add the remaining ingredients and mix well.

3. Reduce heat to low settings and cook for 4 to 6 hours. Before serving, use a paper towel to absorb oil that's risen to the top.

Pineapple Baked Beans

Time: 4 to 8 hours   **Serves: 6 to 8**
Ingredients
1 pound (454 g) ground beef
1 (28-ounce / 794-g) can baked beans
1 (8-ounce / 227-g) can pineapple tidbits, drained
1 (4½-ounce / 128-g) can sliced mushrooms, drained
1 large onion, chopped
1 large green pepper, chopped
½ cup barbecue sauce
2 tablespoons soy sauce
1 clove garlic, minced
½ teaspoon salt
¼ teaspoon pepper

Directions
1. Heat the ground beef in a pan. Place in a crock pot.

2. Add the remaining ingredients and mix well.

3. Cover and cook on low settings for 4 to 8 hours. Serve.

CHAPTER 7

BEVERAGES RECIPES

Mulled Wine

Time: 2 1/4 hours   **Servings: 8**

Ingredients:

1/4 cup light brown sugar

1 small orange, sliced

6 cups sweet red wine

4 whole cloves

2 star anise

1 cup apple cider

1 cinnamon stick

4 cardamom pods, crushed

Directions:

1. Put all the ingredients in your slow cooker.
2. Cover and cook for 2 hours on high settings.
3. Serve warm.

Rosemary Mulled Cider

Time: 3 1/4 hours   **Servings: 6**

Ingredients:

1 cup fresh or frozen cranberries

1 cinnamon stick

2 whole cloves

1 rosemary sprig

4 cups apple cider

2 cups rose wine

1/2 cup white sugar

Directions:

1. Place all the ingredients in your slow cooker.
2. Cover and cook for 3 hours on low settings.
3. Serve the mulled cider warm.

Cranberry Spiced tea

Time: 2 1/4 hours   **Servings: 6**

Ingredients:

1/2 cup white sugar

2 cinnamon stick

4 cups water

2 cardamom pods, crushed

1 lemon, sliced

1 cup strong brewed black tea

1 cup cranberry juice

2 star anise

Directions:

1. Put all the ingredients in your slow cooker.
2. Cook on high settings for 2 hours.
3. Serve the tea warm.

Gingerbread Hot Chocolate

Time: 2 1/4 hours   **Servings: 8**

Ingredients:

1 cup sweetened condensed milk

2 tablespoons cocoa powder

2 cinnamon stick

2 tablespoons maple syrup

6 cups whole milk

1 cup dark chocolate chips

1/2 teaspoon ground ginger

1 pinch salt

Directions:

1. Put all the ingredients in your slow cooker.
2. Cover and cook for 2 hours on high settings.
3. Serve the drink warm.

Gingerbread Mocha Drink

Time: 1 3/4 hours   **Servings: 6**

Ingredients:
1/2 cup sweetened condensed milk
1/4 cup light brown sugar
3 cups whole milk
1/4 teaspoon cardamom powder
2 cups strongly brewed coffee
1/2 teaspoon ground ginger
1/4 teaspoon cinnamon powder

Directions:
1. Put all the ingredients in a slow cooker.
2. Cover and cook for 1 1/2 hours on low settings.
3. Serve the drink warm.

Apple Chai Tea

Time: 4 1/4 hours   **Servings: 8**

Ingredients:
1 star anise
2 whole cloves
1/3 cup white sugar
2 red apples, cored and diced
4 cups brewed black tea
2 cardamom pods, crushed
4 cups fresh apple juice
2 cinnamon stick

Directions:
1. Put all the ingredients in your crock pot.
2. Cook the tea for 4 hours on low settings.
3. Serve the apple chai tea warm.

Salted Caramel Milk Steamer

Time: 2 1/4 hours   **Servings: 6**

Ingredients:
1 cup caramel sauce
1/4 teaspoon salt
4 cups whole milk
1 teaspoon vanilla extract
1 cup heavy cream
1/4 teaspoon ground ginger

Directions:
1. Put all the ingredients in your crock pot.
2. Cover and cook for 2 hours on low settings.
3. Pour the caramel milk steamer into glasses or mugs and serve.

Ginger Pumpkin Latte

Time: 3 1/4 hours   **Servings: 6**

Ingredients:
1 cinnamon stick
1 pinch nutmeg
1 cup brewed coffee
1/4 cup dark brown sugar
4 cups whole milk
1 cup pumpkin puree
1 teaspoon ground ginger

Directions:
1. Put all the ingredients in a slow cooker.
2. Cover and cook for 3 hours on low settings.
3. Serve the drink warm.

Hot Caramel Apple Drink

Time: 2 1/4 hours   **Servings: 8**

Ingredients:
1 cup light rum
6 cups apple cider
1 cup apple liqueur
2 cinnamon stick
1/2 cup caramel syrup
2 red apples, cored and diced

Directions:
1. Combine all the ingredients in your slow cooker.
2. Cover and cook for 2 hours on low settings.
3. Serve warm.

Apple Bourbon Punch

Time: 2 1/4 hours   **Servings: 4**

Ingredients:
2 whole cloves
1/4 cup light brown sugar
3 cups apple cider
2 cinnamon stick
1 cup bourbon
1/2 cup fresh or frozen cranberries

Directions:
1. Mix all the ingredients in your crock pot
2. Cook for 2 hours on low settings.
3. Serve the drink hot.

Spiced White Chocolate

Time: 1 3/4 hours   **Servings: 6**

Ingredients:
1 pinch nutmeg
1 cup white chocolate chips
1 star anise
1/2-inch piece of ginger, sliced
1 cinnamon stick
4 cups whole milk
1 cup sweetened condensed milk

Directions:
1. Mix all the ingredients in your crock pot.
2. Cover and cook for 1 1/2 hours on low settings.
3. Serve the chocolate hot.

Maple Bourbon Mulled Cider

Time: 1 3/4 hours   **Servings: 6**

Ingredients:
2 star anise
1/2 cup fresh apple juice
1/4 cup maple syrup
5 cups apple cider
1/2 cup bourbon

Directions:
1. Combine all the ingredients in your slow cooker.
2. Cover and cook for 1 1/2 hours on low settings.
3. Serve the drink hot.

Autumn Punch

Time: 4 1/4 hours   **Servings: 8**
Ingredients:
1 cup cranberry juice
6 cups red wine
1 cup bourbon
1 ripe pear, cored and sliced
1 cinnamon stick
2 whole cloves
1 vanilla bean, split in half lengthwise
2 red apples, cored and diced

Directions:
1. Mix all the ingredients in your slow cooker.
2. Cover and cook for 4 hours on low settings.
3. Serve hot or cool.

Boozy Hot Chocolate

Time: 4 1/4 hours   **Servings: 6**
Ingredients:
1 cup dark chocolate chips
2 tablespoons maple syrup
1 cinnamon stick
1/2 cup dark rum
4 cups whole milk
1 cup sweetened condensed milk

Directions:
1. Combine all the ingredients in your slow cooker.
2. Cover and cook for 4 hours on low settings.
3. Serve the hot chocolate.

Hot Spicy Apple Cider

Time: 3 1/4 hours   **Servings: 6**
Ingredients:
1 star anise
2 cinnamon stick
5 cups apple cider
1 cup white rum
1 orange, sliced
1/4 teaspoon chili powder

Directions:
1. Mix all the ingredients in your crock pot.
2. Cover and cook for 3 hours on low settings.
3. Serve the apple cider warm.

Vanilla Latte

Time: 2 1/4 hours   **Servings: 6**
Ingredients:
1/4 cup sweetened condensed milk
2 cups brewed coffee
1 vanilla pod, split in half lengthwise
4 cups whole milk

Directions:
1. Mix all the ingredients in your crock pot.
2. Cover and cook for 2 hours on low settings.
3. Serve the vanilla latte warm.

Apple Ginger Delight

Time: 1 3/4 hours   **Servings: 6**

Ingredients:

1/2 cup bourbon
1-inch piece of ginger, sliced
1 teaspoon dark molasses
4 cups apple cider
1 cup ginger beer
1/4 cup light brown sugar

Directions:

1. Mix all the ingredients in your slow cooker.
2. Cover and cook on low settings for 1 1/2 hours.
3. Serve the apple ginger delight hot.

Citrus Bourbon Cocktail

Time: 3 1/4 hours   **Servings: 6**

Ingredients:

1/4 cup white sugar
1 cinnamon stick
1 small grapefruit, sliced
1 small orange, sliced
1 lemon, sliced
4 cups apple cider
1 cup fresh orange juice
1 cup bourbon

Directions:

1. Mix all the ingredients in your crock pot.
2. Cover and cook on low settings for 3 hours.
3. Serve warm.

Eggnog Latte

Time: 2 1/4 hours   **Servings: 6**

Ingredients:

1 cup whole milk
1/4 cup light brown sugar
2 cups brewed coffe3
3 cups eggnog
1 teaspoon vanilla extract
1 pinch nutmeg

Directions:

1. Mix all the ingredients in your slow cooker.
2. Cook on low settings for 2 hours.
3. Serve warm or cool.

Lemonade Cider

Time: 1 1/2 hours   **Servings: 6**

Ingredients:

1 large lemon, sliced
5 cups apple cider
1/4 cup honey
1 cup ginger beer

Directions:

1. Mix all the ingredients in your slow cooker.
2. Cover and cook for 1 1/4 hours on low settings.
3. Serve the cider warm or cool.

Spiced Pumpkin Toddy

Time: 3 1/4 hours   **Servings: 6**
Ingredients:
2 cups water
1/4 cup maple syrup
1 cinnamon stick
1/2 cup pumpkin puree
1 cup bourbon
2 cups apple cider
2 cardamom pods, crushed
1 star anise
2 orange peels

Directions:
1. Mix all the ingredients in your slow cooker.
2. Cover and cook for 3 hours on low settings.
3. Serve the drink warm.

Raspberry Hot Chocolate

Time: 2 1/4 hours   **Servings: 8**
Ingredients:
1 pinch salt
1 cup heavy cream
6 cups whole milk
1/4 cup cocoa powder
1 cup sweetened condensed milk
1/2 cup seedless raspberry jam

Directions:
1. Mix all the ingredients in your crock pot.
2. Cover and cook for 2 hours on low settings.
3. Serve the chocolate hot.

Nutella Hot Chocolate

Time: 4 1/4 hours   **Servings: 6**
Ingredients:
1 cinnamon stick
5 cups whole milk
1/4 cup heavy cream
3/4 cup Nutella spread

Directions:
1. Combine all the ingredients in your slow cooker.
2. Cover and cook for 4 hours on low settings.
3. Serve the chocolate hot.

Mulled Cranberry Punch

Time: 3 1/4 hours   **Servings: 8**
Ingredients:
3 cups apple cider
1/2 cup bourbon
1 star anise
1/2 cup maple syrup
4 cups cranberry juice
1 cup fresh or frozen cranberries
2 whole cloves
1 cinnamon stick

Directions:
1. Mix all the ingredients in your crock pot.
2. Cover and cook for 3 hours on low settings.
3. Serve warm or cool.

Citrus Green Tea

Time: 1 3/4 hours   **Servings: 6**
Ingredients:
1 lemon, sliced
1/4 cup honey
5 cups brewed green tea
1 cup fresh orange juice
1/2-inch piece of ginger, sliced

Directions:
1. Mix all the ingredients in your slow cooker.
2. Cover and cook on low settings for 1 1/2 hours.
3. Serve the green tea warm or cool.

Mulled Pink Wine

Time: 2 1/4 hours   **Servings: 6**
Ingredients:
1/4 cup honey
2 cardamom pods, crushed
6 cups rose wine
1 cup fresh raspberries

Directions:
1. Mix all the ingredients in your slow cooker.
2. Cover and cook on low settings for 2 hours.
3. Serve the wine warm.

Whiskey Pumpkin Drink

Time: 2 1/4 hours   **Servings: 6**
Ingredients:
3 cups water
1 cinnamon stick
1/4 cup maple syrup
1 cup ginger ale
1 cup whiskey
1/2 cup pumpkin puree

Directions:
1. Combine all the ingredients in a slow cooker
2. Cook for 2 hours on low settings.
3. Serve the drink warm or cool.

Black Tea Punch

Time: 4 1/4 hours   **Servings: 8**
Ingredients:
1 lemon, sliced
2 cups apple juice
1 orange, sliced
4 cups brewed black tea
1/4 cup white sugar
2 cups cranberry juice
1 cinnamon stick

Directions:
1. Mix all the ingredients in your slow cooker.
2. Cover and cook for 4 hours on low settings.
3. Serve warm.

Cherry Cider

Time: 1 3/4 hours   **Servings: 8**
Ingredients:
1 star anise
2 cinnamon stick
6 cups apple cider
2 cups cherry juice

Directions:
1. Mix all the ingredients in your slow cooker.
2. Cook on low settings for 1 1/2 hours.
3. Serve the cider warm.

Spiced Coffee

Time: 2 1/4 hours   **Servings: 6**
Ingredients:
1/4 cup white sugar
1 cinnamon stick
2 whole cloves
2 cardamom pods, crushed
1 star anise
6 cups brewed coffee
1/4 cup chocolate syrup

Directions:
1. Mix the ingredients in a slow cooker
2. Cook for 2 hours on low settings.
2. Serve warm.

Chocolate Hot Coffee

Time: 3 1/4 hours   **Servings: 6**
Ingredients:
1/2 cup chocolate syrup
1/2 cup heavy cream
4 cups brewed coffee
1 cup dark chocolate chips

Directions:
1. Mix all the ingredients in your crock pot.
2. Cover and cook for 3 hours on low settings.
3. Serve the coffee hot.

Kahlua Coffee

Time: 1 1/4 hours   **Servings: 6**
Ingredients:
2 cups water
1/4 cup Kahlua
2 cups whole milk
2 teaspoons instant powder
1 teaspoon vanilla extract
1/4 cup white sugar
2 cups heavy cream

Directions:
1. Mix all the ingredients in your slow cooker.
2. Cover and cook on low settings for 1 hour.
3. Serve the coffee warm.

Peachy Cider

Time: 4 1/4 hours   **Servings: 6**

Ingredients:

1 star anise
2 cups apple cider
1 cinnamon stick
2 cups peach nectar
2 tablespoons light brown sugar
2 cups apple juice
1 pinch nutmeg
2 cardamom pods, crushed

Directions:

1. Mix all the ingredients in your slow cooker.
2. Cover and cook for 4 hours on low settings.
3. Serve warm.

Ginger Tea Drink

Time: 1 1/4 hours   **Servings: 6**

Ingredients:

1 lemon, sliced
1/4 cup honey
1-inch piece of ginger, sliced
6 cups water
6 green tea bags

Directions:

1. Combine all the ingredients in a slow cooker.
2. Cover and cook for 1 hour on low settings.
3. Remove the lemon slices and tea bags and pour the drink in mugs.
4. Serve warm.

Pomegranate Cider

Time: 2 1/4 hours   **Servings: 6**

Ingredients:

1 star anise
1 small orange, sliced
4 cups apple cider
1 1/2 cups pomegranate juiced
1/4 cup brown sugar
1/2 cup ginger ale
1 cinnamon stick

Directions:

1. Combine all the ingredients in your crock pot.
2. Cover and cook for 2 hours on low settings.
3. Serve warm.

Spiced Lemon Cider Punch

Time: 2 1/4 hours   **Servings: 6**

Ingredients:

1 cup cranberry juice
1/4 cup lemon juice
4 cups apple cider
1/4 cup honey
2 cardamom pods, crushed
1 cup water
1 lemon, sliced

Directions:

1. Mix the cranberry juice, lemon juice, apple cider, water, lemon slices, honey, and cardamom pods in your slow cooker.
2. Cover and cook for 2 hours on low settings.
3. Serve warm.

Brandied Mulled Wine

Time: 1 3/4 hours   **Servings: 8**
Ingredients:
2 whole cloves
2 cardamom pods, crushed
1/4 cup maple syrup
1 cinnamon stick
7 cups dry white wine
1 cup brandy
1 star anise

Directions:
1. Combine all the ingredients in your crock pot.
2. Cover and cook for 1 1/2 hours on low settings.
3. Serve warm.

Caramel Hot Chocolate

Time: 4 1/4 hours   **Servings: 6**
Ingredients:
1 pinch salt
1 cup dark chocolate chips
1 cup evaporated milk
3/4 cup caramel sauce
4 cups whole milk

Directions:
1. Mix all the ingredients in your slow cooker.
2. Cover and cook for 4 hours on low settings.
3. Serve the chocolate warm and hot.

Hot Whiskey Sour

Time: 2 1/4 hours   **Servings: 6**
Ingredients:
1 tablespoon honey
1/2 cup white sugar
4 cups water
1 cup whiskey
1/2 cup lemon juice

Directions:
1. Combine all the ingredients in your crock pot.
2. Cover and cook for 2 hours on low settings.
3. Serve warm.

Hot Marmalade Cider

Time: 1 1/4 hours   **Servings: 6**
Ingredients:
1 orange, sliced
1/4 cup orange marmalade
5 cups apple cider
1 cup fresh orange juice

Directions:
1. Combine all the ingredients in your crock pot.
2. Cover and cook for 1 hour on high settings.
3. Serve warm.

Peppermint Hot Chocolate

Time: 1 3/4 hours　　　**Servings: 6**
Ingredients:
1 cup dark chocolate
1 pinch salt
4 cups whole milk
1 cup heavy cream
1 tablespoon cocoa powder
1 teaspoon peppermint extract

Directions:
1. Combine all the ingredients in your slow cooker.
2. Cover and cook for 1 1/2 hours on low settings.
3. Serve warm.

Orange Brandy Hot Toddy

Time: 2 1/4 hours　　　**Servings: 6**
Ingredients:
1 cup brandy
1 cinnamon stick
4 cups brewed black tea
1/2-inch piece of ginger, sliced
2 orange slices
1 cup fresh orange juice
1/4 cup honey

Directions:
1. Mix all the ingredients in your slow cooker.
2. Cover and cook for 2 hours on low settings.
3. Serve the drink hot.

Spicy Mulled Red Wine

Time: 4 1/4 hours　　　**Servings: 6**
Ingredients:
1 star anise
2 cardamom pods, crushed
1/2 bay leaf
1/2 cup white sugar
1 cinnamon stick
6 cups red wine
1 teaspoon peppercorns

Directions:
1. Mix all the ingredients in your slow cooker.
2. Cover and cook for 4 hours on low settings.
3. Serve warm.

Lemon Lime Jasmine Tea

Time: 1 1/4 hours　　　**Servings: 6**
Ingredients:
1 lemon, sliced
1 lime, sliced
6 cups water
1/2 cup white sugar
2 tablespoons jasmine buds

Directions:
1. Mix all the ingredients in your crock pot.
2. Cook for 1 hour on high settings.
3. Serve the tea hot.

Party Cranberry Punch

Time: 4 1/4 hours   **Servings: 6**
Ingredients:
1/2 cup fresh or frozen cranberries
1 small orange, sliced
2 cups cranberry juice
2 tablespoons honey
2 cinnamon sticks
4 cups apple cider
1 red apple, cored and sliced
1 peach, pitted and sliced

Directions:
1. Combine all the ingredients in your crock pot.
2. Cook for 4 hours on low settings
3. Serve the drink warm.

Caramel Cider

Time: 1 1/4 hours   **Servings: 6**
Ingredients:
1 cinnamon stick
1/2 cup water
4 cups apple cider
1/2 cups white sugar
1 cup fresh orange juice

Directions:
1. Heat the sugar in a pan until it has an amber color. Add water and cook for 2 minutes until the sugar is fully melted.
2. Mix the caramel sauce with the remaining ingredients in your crock pot.
3. Cook for 1 hour on high settings.
4. Serve warm.

Hot Cranberry Toddy

Time: 4 1/4 hours   **Servings: 8**
Ingredients:
1/2 cup fresh or frozen cranberries
1/4 cup dark rum
1/4 cup light brown sugar
6 cups apple cider
2 cups cranberry juice

Directions:
1. Combine all the ingredients in your crock pot.
2. Cook for 4 hours on low settings.
3. Serve warm.

The Ultimate Hot Chocolate

Time: 4 1/4 hours   **Servings: 6**
Ingredients:
1 pinch salt
1 cup sweetened condensed milk
1 cup heavy cream
1 cup dark chocolate chips
4 cups whole milk
1 tablespoon cocoa powder
Mini marshmallows for serving

Directions:
1. Combine all the ingredients in your crock pot.
2. Cover and cook for 4 hours on low settings.
3. Serve the drink hot and also top with marshmallows.

Buttered Hot Rum

Time: 4 1/4 hours   **Servings: 6**
Ingredients:
1/4 cup butter
1 cup dark rum
2 cinnamon stick
4 cups water
1 cup dark brown sugar
1 whole clove

Directions:
1. Combine the butter, cinnamon, water, sugar, and whole clove in your slow cooker.
2. Cook for 4 hours on low settings.
3. Add the rum and serve immediately.

Irish Cream Coffee

Time: 3 1/4 hours   **Servings: 4**
Ingredients
1/2 cup heavy cream
1/4 cup heavy cream
1 tablespoon cocoa powder
3 cups brewed coffee
1/2 cup Irish cream liqueur

Directions:
1. Combine all the ingredients in your crock pot.
2. Cook for 3 hours on low settings.
3. Serve warm.

CHAPTER 8

PORK RECIPES

Brazilian Pork Stew

Time: 7 1/4 hours   **Servings: 6**

Ingredients:
2 sweet onions, chopped
4 bacon slices, chopped
1/2 pound dried black beans
1 1/2 pounds pork shoulder, cubed
2 cups chicken stock
Salt and pepper
2 bay leaves
1 teaspoon white wine vinegar
1/2 teaspoon ground coriander
4 garlic cloves, chopped
1 teaspoon cumin seeds

Directions:
1. Mix the beans and pork with the remaining ingredients in your crock pot.
2. Add salt and pepper and cover.
3. Cook on low settings for 7 hours.
4. Serve warm.

BBQ Pork Ribs

Time: 11 1/4 hours   **Servings: 8**

Ingredients:
1 celery stalk, sliced
1 tablespoon Dijon mustard
1 teaspoon chili powder
1/4 cup chicken stock
Salt and pepper
5 pounds pork short ribs
2 cups BBQ sauce
1 large onion, sliced
1 tablespoon brown sugar
4 garlic cloves, minced

Directions:
1. Place the pork short ribs, BBQ sauce, onion, celery and mustard, and also chili, sugar, garlic and stock in your slow cooker.
2. Add salt and pepper and cook on low settings for 11 hours.
3. Serve warm.

Apple Bourbon Pork Chops

Time: 8 1/4 hours   **Servings: 6**

Ingredients:
1 thyme sprig
1 rosemary sprig
6 pork chops
1/4 cup bourbon
1/2 cup chicken stock
4 red apples, cored and sliced
1/2 cup applesauce
Salt and pepper

Directions:
1. Mix the pork chops with salt and pepper.
2. Place the apples, applesauce, bourbon, stock, thyme and rosemary in your slow cooker.
3. Put the pork chops on top and cook on low settings for 8 hours.
4. Serve the pork chops with the sauce.

Red Wine Braised Pork Ribs

Time: 8 1/4 hours   **Servings: 8**

Ingredients:
1 teaspoon chili powder
1 teaspoon cumin powder
1 tablespoon molasses
1 teaspoon salt
1 cup BBQ sauce
2 tablespoons olive oil
1 teaspoon dried thyme
5 pounds pork short ribs
4 tablespoons brown sugar
1 cup red wine

Directions:
1. Combine the brown sugar, molasses, olive oil, chili powder, cumin powder, thyme and salt in a bowl.
2. Spread this mixture over the pork ribs and coat the meat well with the spice.
3. Put it in your crock pot.
4. Add the BBQ sauce and red wine and cook on low settings for 8 hours.
5. Serve warm.

Onion Pork Tenderloin

Time: 8 1/4 hours   **Servings: 6**
Ingredients:
1/2 cup chicken stock
Salt and pepper
1 thyme sprig
2 tablespoons canola oil
3 large sweet onions, sliced
2 pounds pork tenderloin
6 bacon slices
1/2 cup white wine

Directions:
1. Heat the oil in a clean pan and add the onions. Cook for 10 minutes until softened and a little bit caramelized.
2. Place the onions in your crock pot and add the remaining ingredients.
3. Add salt and pepper and cook on low settings for 8 hours.

Fennel Infused Pork Ham

Time: 6 1/4 hours   **Servings: 8**
Ingredients:
1 orange, zested and juiced
1/2 cup white wine
4-5 pounds piece of pork ham
1 thyme sprig
Salt and pepper
2 fennel bulbs, sliced
1 cup chicken stock
2 bay leaves

Directions:
1. Mix the fennel, orange zest, orange juice, white wine, chicken stock, bay leaves and thyme in your crock pot.
2. Add salt and pepper and place the ham on top.
3. Cook on low settings for 6 hours.
4. Serve warm.

Country Style Pork Ribs

Time: 6 1/4 hours   **Servings: 4**
Ingredients:
1 teaspoon garlic powder
1 cup pineapple juice
1 tablespoon brown sugar
3 pounds short pork ribs
1 teaspoon salt
1 teaspoon dried thyme

Directions:
1. Sprinkle the pork ribs with salt, garlic powder, brown sugar and thyme and place into your slow cooker.
2. Add the pineapple juice and cook on low settings for 6 hours.
3. Serve warm.

Chili Verde

Time: 7 1/4 hours   **Servings: 8**
Ingredients:
1 teaspoon dried oregano
1 teaspoon cumin powder
1 large onion, chopped
4 garlic cloves, chopped
1/2 teaspoon smoked paprika
2 green chilis, chopped
1/4 teaspoon chili powder
1 bunch cilantro, chopped
1 1/2 cups chicken stock
Salt and pepper
2 pounds pork shoulder, cubed
2 tablespoons canola oil
2 pounds tomatillos, peeled and chopped

Directions:
1. Heat the oil in a clean pan and add the pork shoulder. Cook for a few minutes until golden then place it in your slow cooker.
2. Add the remaining ingredients and sprinkle with salt and pepper.
3. Cook on low settings for 7 hours.
4. Serve warm.

Mexican Pork Roast

Time: 8 1/4 hours **Servings: 6**

Ingredients:
1 bay leaf
1 cup chicken stock
Salt and pepper
2 carrots, sliced
2 celery stalks, sliced
2 pounds pork shoulder, cubed
1 teaspoon smoked paprika
1/2 teaspoon cumin powder
1 can fire roasted tomatoes
1 large onion, chopped

Directions:
1. Mix the pork shoulder, tomatoes, carrots, celery, onion, paprika, cumin powder, bay leaf, stock, salt and pepper.
2. Cook on low settings for 8 hours.
3. Serve warm.

Balsamic Roasted Pork

Time: 6 1/4 hours **Servings: 8**

Ingredients:
1 teaspoon five-spice powder
1 teaspoon hot sauce
1/4 cup balsamic vinegar
1 teaspoon garlic powder
2 tablespoons honey
Salt and pepper
4 pounds pork shoulder, cubed
2 tablespoons brown sugar

Directions:
1. Combine the sugar, ginger, five-spice powder, honey and hot sauce in a bowl. Pour the mixture over the pork.
2. Place the pork in the crock pot and add the vinegar.
3. Add salt and pepper and cook on low settings for 6 hours.
4. Serve the pork warm with your favorite side dish.

Pineapple Cranberry Pork Ham

Time: 7 1/4 hours **Servings: 6**

Ingredients:
1 bay leaf
1 star anise
Salt and pepper
1 cup pineapple juice
1/2 teaspoon chili powder
2-3 pounds piece of smoked ham
1 cup cranberry sauce
1/2 teaspoon cumin powder
1 cinnamon stick

Directions:
1. Combine the cranberry sauce, pineapple juice, chili powder, cumin powder, cinnamon, star anise, and bay leaf in a crock pot.
2. Place the ham in the crock pot and add salt and pepper if needed.
3. Cook on low settings for 7 hours.
4. Serve the pork warm with your favorite side dish.

Italian Style Pork Shoulder

Time: 7 1/4 hours **Servings: 6**

Ingredients:
4 garlic cloves, chopped
2 celery stalks, sliced
2 pounds pork shoulder
1/4 cup white wine
Salt and pepper
1 teaspoon dried thyme
1 teaspoon dried basil
1 thyme sprig
1 large onion, sliced
2 ripe tomatoes, peeled and diced

Directions:
1. Mix all the ingredients in your crock pot and add enough salt and pepper.
2. Cover and cook on low settings for 7 hours.
3. Serve the pork warm with your favorite side dish.

Apple Butter Short Ribs

Time: 8 1/4 hours   **Servings: 8**
Ingredients:
2 tablespoons brown sugar
1 teaspoon garlic powder
Salt and pepper
1/2 teaspoon chili powder
1/2 cup BBQ sauce
1 cup vegetable stock
4 pounds pork short ribs
1 cup apple butter
1 teaspoon onion powder

Directions:
1. Combine the apple butter, sugar, garlic powder, onion powder, chili powder, BBQ sauce and stock in your slow cooker.
2. Add the ribs, salt, and pepper.
3. Cover and cook on low settings for 8 hours.
4. Serve warm.

Ginger Beer Pork Ribs

Time: 6 3/4 hours   **Servings: 6**
Ingredients:
1/2 cup ketchup
Salt and pepper
1 tablespoon Worcestershire sauce
2-3 pounds pork short ribs
1/2 teaspoon smoked paprika
1 tablespoon brown sugar
1 cup ginger beer
1 tablespoon Dijon mustard

Directions:
1. Put all the necessary ingredients in your crock pot.
2. Add salt and pepper.
3. Cook on low settings for 6 1/2 hours.
4. Serve the pork warm with your favorite side dish.

Teriyaki Pork Tenderloin

Time: 7 1/4 hours   **Servings: 6**
Ingredients:
1/4 cup ketchup
1 onion, chopped
2 pounds pork tenderloin
1/4 cup soy sauce
1 tablespoon hot sauce
1/4 cup chicken stock or water
4 garlic cloves, minced
1 tablespoon smooth peanut butter
1 tablespoon brown sugar

Directions:
1. Place the soy sauce, ketchup, onion, peanut butter, sugar, hot sauce, garlic and stock in your crock pot.
2. Add the pork tenderloin.
3. Cook on low settings for 7 hours.
4. Serve the pork warm with your favorite side dish.

Sauerkraut Cumin Pork

Time: 6 1/4 hours   **Servings: 6**
Ingredients:
1 large onion, chopped
2 carrots, grated
1 1/2 pounds pork shoulder, cubed
1 1/2 pounds sauerkraut, shredded
1 cup chicken stock
1 bay leaf
1 1/2 teaspoons cumin seeds
1/4 teaspoon red pepper flakes
Salt and pepper

Directions:
1. Put all the necessary ingredients in your crock pot.
2. Add salt and pepper
3. Cook on low settings for 6 hours.
3. Serve warm.

Herbed Roasted Pork

Time: 6 1/4 hours   **Servings: 6**
Ingredients:
1/2 cup chopped cilantro
4 basil leaves
1/2 cup grated Parmesan
Salt and pepper
1 lemon, juiced
2 pounds pork tenderloin
1 cup chopped parsley
1/4 cup pine nuts
1/2 cup chicken stock.

Directions:
1. Combine the parsley, cilantro, basil, pine nuts, stock, cheese, lemon juice, salt and pepper in a food processor and blend until smooth.
2. Mix the pork tenderloin with the herbed mixture and cook on low settings for 6 hours.
3. Add Parmesan and serve with your favorite side dish.

Chili BBQ Ribs

Time: 8 1/2 hours   **Servings: 8**
Ingredients:
1 1/2 teaspoons chili powder
1 teaspoon cumin powder
6 pounds pork short ribs
2 cups BBQ sauce
1 teaspoon Worcestershire sauce
2 tablespoons brown sugar
2 tablespoons red wine vinegar
Salt and pepper

Directions:
1. Combine the BBQ sauce, cumin powder, chili powder, sugar, vinegar, Worcestershire sauce, salt, and pepper in a slow cooker.
2. Add the short ribs and stir until well coated.
3. Cover and cook on low settings for 8 1/4 hours.
4. Serve warm.

Lemon Roasted Pork Tenderloin

Time: 7 1/4 hours   **Servings: 6**
Ingredients:
Salt and pepper
1 teaspoon black pepper kernels
1 cup canola oil
2 pounds pork tenderloin
1 lemon, sliced
1 cup vegetable stock

Directions:
1. Mix all the ingredients in your slow cooker.
2. Add salt and pepper and cook on low settings for 7 hours.
3. Serve warm.

Sour Cream Pork Chops

Time: 6 1/4 hours   **Servings: 6**
Ingredients:
1/2 cup chicken stock
Salt and pepper
2 green onions, chopped
6 pork chops, bone in
1 cup sour cream
2 tablespoons chopped parsley
Directions:
1. Place the pork chops, sour cream, stock, onions and parsley in your crock pot.
2. Add salt and pepper and cook on low settings for 6 hours.
3. Serve warm and top with plenty of sauce.

Hawaiian Pork Roast

Time: 8 1/4 hours   **Servings: 8**
Ingredients:
1 rosemary sprig
1 bay leaf
Salt and pepper
1 cup pineapple juice
1 cup frozen cranberries
4 pounds pork roast
1 mango, peeled and cubed
2 tablespoons red wine vinegar

Directions:
1. Place the pork roast, mango cubes, pineapple juice, cranberries, vinegar, bay leaf and rosemary sprig in the slow cooker.
2. Add salt and pepper
3. Cook on low settings for 8 hours.
4. Serve warm.

Black Bean Pork Stew

Time: 9 1/4 hours   **Servings: 10**
Ingredients:
1 pound dried black beans
1 can fire roasted tomatoes
2 red onions, chopped
4 garlic cloves, chopped
1 teaspoon dried oregano
1 teaspoon dried basil
1 teaspoon cumin powder
3 pounds pork roast, cubed
Salt and pepper
1 teaspoon chili powder
2 cups chicken stock
2 chipotle peppers, chopped

Directions:
1. Put the onions, garlic, black beans, tomatoes, stock, chipotle peppers, oregano, basil, cumin powder, chili powder and pork roast in a slow cooker.
2. Add salt and pepper
3. Cook on low settings for 9 hours.
4. Serve the stew warm and fresh or chilled.

Honey Glazed Pork Ribs

Time: 8 1/4 hours   **Servings: 6**
Ingredients:
2 tablespoons honey
1 star anise
1/4 cup BBQ sauce
1 tablespoon maple syrup
1 cup chicken stock
1 teaspoon salt
4 pounds pork ribs
2 tablespoons honey and mustard
1/2 teaspoon cayenne pepper

Directions:
1. Put the mustard, honey, maple syrup, star anise, BBQ sauce, stock, salt and cayenne pepper in your slow cooker.
2. Add the pork ribs and mix them with the mixture.
3. Cover and cook on low settings for 8 hours.
4. Serve warm.

Mango Flavored Pulled Pork

Time: 7 1/4 hours   **Servings: 8**
Ingredients:
1 tablespoon balsamic vinegar
1 cup BBQ sauce
1 cup chicken stock
1 chipotle pepper, chopped
1 ripe mango, peeled and diced
1/4 cup bourbon
Salt and pepper
4 pounds pork roast, cut into large pieces

Directions:
1. Put all the necessary ingredients in your crock pot.
2. Add salt and pepper and cook on low settings for 7 hours.
3. Serve warm.

Pork Sausage Stew

Time: 6 1/4 hours   **Servings: 8**

Ingredients:
2 carrots, diced
1 celery stalk, diced
1 cup red lentils
2/3 cup brown lentils
1 bay leaf
1 chipotle pepper, chopped
Salt and pepper
1 cup diced tomatoes
2 garlic cloves, chopped
1-pound fresh pork sausages, sliced
1 large onion, finely chopped
1 tablespoon tomato paste
3 cups chicken stock
2 tablespoons chopped parsley for serving

Directions:
1. Place the pork sausages, onion, carrots, celery, garlic, lentils, tomatoes, tomato paste, stock, bay leaf and chipotle pepper in the slow cooker.
2. Add salt and pepper
3. Cook on low settings for 6 hours.
4. Serve warm and top with chopped parsley.

Sweet Potato Pork Stew

Time: 6 1/4 hours   **Servings: 6**

Ingredients:
2 shallots, chopped
Salt and pepper
2 red apples, peeled and cubed
1 pinch nutmeg
2 tablespoons tomato paste
2 cups chicken stock
1 teaspoon Dijon mustard
1 1/2 pounds pork tenderloin, cubed
3 large sweet potatoes, peeled and cubed

Directions:
1. Put the pork, sweet potatoes, shallots, apples, nutmeg, mustard, tomato paste and stock in your slow cooker.
2. Add salt and pepper
3. Cook on low settings for 6 hours.
4. Serve warm or re-heated.

Roasted Bell Pepper Pork Stew

Time: 5 1/4 hours   **Servings: 6**

Ingredients:
1 cup chicken stock
1 cup tomato sauce
Salt and pepper
1 jar roasted bell pepper, drained and chopped
4 garlic cloves, chopped
1 large onion, chopped
1/2 teaspoon red pepper flakes
2 pounds pork tenderloin, cubed
2 tablespoons canola oil

Directions:
1. Heat the oil in a clean pan and add the pork. Cook for a few minutes until golden. Place it in your slow cooker.
2. Add the remaining ingredients and sprinkle with salt and pepper.
3. Cover and cook on low settings for 5 hours.
4. Serve warm.

Red Chile Pulled Pork

Time: 7 1/4 hours   **Servings: 8**

Ingredients:
Salt and pepper
2 red chilis, seeded and chopped
1 large onion, chopped
4 pounds pork roast
1 cup tomato sauce
1 cup red salsa

Directions:
1. Mix all the ingredients in your slow cooker.
2. Add salt and pepper
3. Cook on low settings for 7 hours.
4. When done, shred the pork into fine threads using two forks.
5. Serve warm.

Blackberry Pork Tenderloin

Time: 7 1/4 hours   **Servings: 6**
Ingredients:
2 red onions, sliced
1/2 cup chicken stock
Salt and pepper
1/2 teaspoon dried sage
1/2 teaspoon dried oregano
2 tablespoons honey
2 pounds pork tenderloin
2 cups fresh blackberries
1 tablespoon balsamic vinegar

Directions:
1. Mix all the ingredients in your crock pot.
2. Add salt and pepper and cover.
3. Cook on low settings for 7 hours.
4. When done, slice the pork and serve it warm.

Havana Style Pork Roast

Time: 6 1/4 hours   **Servings: 6**
Ingredients:
1 celery stalk, sliced
4 garlic cloves, chopped
2 pounds pork roast
1 onion, sliced
1/2 cup fresh orange juice
1/4 teaspoon chili powder
1 bay leaf
Salt and pepper
1 lemon, zested and juiced
1 teaspoon cumin powder

Directions:
1. Mix all the ingredients in your slow cooker.
2. Add salt and pepper and cook on low settings for 6 hours.
3. Serve warm.

Creamy Dijon Pork Shoulder

Time: 7 1/4 hours   **Servings: 8**
Ingredients:
4 garlic cloves, chopped
1 large onion, chopped
2 tablespoons canola oil
4 pounds pork tenderloin
2 cups sliced mushrooms
1 can condensed cream of mushroom soup
Salt and pepper
2 tablespoons Dijon mustard

Directions:
1. Heat the canola oil in a clean pan. Mix the pork with salt and pepper and transfer it into the hot oil then fry.
2. Place the meat in your slow cooker.
3. Add the remaining ingredients and sprinkle with salt and pepper.
4. Cook on low settings for 7 hours.
5. Serve the pork warm and top with the creamy sauce found in the pot.

Marsala Pork Chops

Time: 6 1/4 hours   **Servings: 6**
Ingredients:
6 pork chops
2 tablespoons all-purpose flour
1 teaspoon garlic powder
1 onion, sliced
4 garlic cloves, chopped
2 cups sliced mushrooms
1/2 cup Marsala wine
1 can condensed cream of mushroom soup
Salt and pepper
Directions:
1. Sprinkle the pork chopped with salt and pepper then add the flour.
2. Place the pork chops in your slow cooker and add the remaining ingredients.
3. Sprinkle with salt and pepper
4. Cook on low settings for 6 hours.
5. Serve the pork chops and the sauce formed in the pot warm.

Slow Cooked Pork in Tomato Sauce

Time: 8 1/4 hours   **Servings: 8**
Ingredients:
Salt and pepper
2 tablespoons tomato paste
1 teaspoon cumin seeds
1 teaspoon fennel seeds
1 teaspoon garlic powder
2 bay leaves
4 pounds pork tenderloin
2 cups tomato sauce
1 teaspoon celery seeds
Directions:
1. Mix all the ingredients in your slow cooker.
2. Add salt and pepper
3. Cook the pork on low settings for 8 hours.
4. Serve the pork warm with your favorite side dish.

Sweet and Sour Pork Chops

Time: 3 1/4 hours   **Servings: 6**
Ingredients:
1/4 teaspoon cumin seeds
Salt and pepper
2 garlic cloves, chopped
1 celery stalk, sliced
1 cup apple cider
6 pork chops
1 large onion, sliced
2 tablespoons balsamic vinegar
2 tablespoons honey
1 bay leaf

Directions:
1. Mix the onion, garlic, celery, vinegar, honey, cider, cumin seeds and bay leaf in a crock pot.
2. Mix the pork chops with salt and pepper and place them in the crock pot.
3. Cook on high settings for 3 hours.
4. Serve warm.

Tomato Sauce Pork Roast

Time: 3 1/4 hours   **Servings: 4**
Ingredients:
1/4 teaspoon cayenne pepper
Salt and pepper
1/2 cup tomato sauce
1/2 cup chicken stock
2 pounds pork roast, cubed
2 tablespoons canola oil
2 tablespoons tomato paste

Directions:
1. Combine all the necessary ingredients in your slow cooker.
2. Add salt and pepper and cook on high settings for 3 hours.
3. Serve the pork roast warm and fresh with your favorite side dish.

Bacon Potato Stew

Time: 6 1/2 hours   **Servings: 6**
Ingredients:
2 carrots, diced
1 celery stalk, diced
2 sweet potatoes, peeled and cubed
1 pound Yukon gold potatoes, peeled and cubed
2 red bell peppers, cored and diced
1/2 teaspoon chili powder
1 cup diced tomatoes
Salt and pepper
1 cup diced bacon
1 large onion, chopped
1/2 teaspoon cumin seeds
2 cups chicken stock

Directions:
1. Heat a clean pan and add the bacon. Cook until crisp then place in the slow cooker.
2. Add the remaining ingredients and also salt and pepper.
3. Cook on low settings for 6 hours.
4. Serve warm.

Miso Braised Pork

Time: 7 1/4 hours   **Servings: 8**
Ingredients:
1 tablespoon grated ginger
1 cup vegetable stock
1 lemongrass stalk, crushed
2 tablespoons canola oil
4 pounds pork shoulder
6 garlic cloves, minced
2 tablespoons miso paste

Directions:
1. Combine the garlic, ginger, canola oil, miso paste, stock and lemongrass in your crock pot.
2. Put the pork shoulder in the crock pot and cover.
3. Cook on low settings for 7 hours.
4. Serve the pork warm with your favorite side dish.

Red Bean Pork Stew

Time: 3 1/4 hours   **Servings: 6**
Ingredients:
1 chorizo link, sliced
1 red onion, chopped
1 teaspoon hot sauce
4 bacon slices, chopped
4 garlic cloves, chopped
Salt and pepper
1 bay leaf
1 can fire roasted tomatoes
2 cups vegetable stock
1/2 pound dried red beans, rinsed
1 1/2 pounds pork roast, cubed

Directions:
1. Place the beans, pork roast, chorizo, bacon, garlic, onion and hot sauce in your slow cooker.
2. Add the tomatoes, stock, bay leaf, salt and pepper.
3. Cook on high settings for 3 hours.
4. Serve warm.

Smoked Ham and Lima Bean Stew

Time: 6 1/4 hours   **Servings: 6**
Ingredients:
Salt and pepper
2 cups water
1 cup chicken stock
2 cups diced smoked ham
1 pound dried lima beans
1/4 teaspoon garlic powder
1/4 teaspoon onion powder
1 cup diced tomatoes
1 teaspoon Cajun seasoning
1/4 teaspoon cayenne pepper

Directions:
1. Combine the ham, beans, water, stock, tomatoes, Cajun seasoning, garlic powder, onion powder, cayenne pepper, salt and pepper in your slow cooker.
2. Cook on low settings for 6 hours.
3. Serve warm.

Spiced Plum Pork Chops

Time: 7 1/4 hours   **Servings: 6**
Ingredients:
1/2 cup apple cider
2 tablespoons brown sugar
1 star anise
1 bay leaf
2 whole cloves
Salt and pepper
1/2 cup chicken stock
6 pork chops
6 plums, pitted and chopped
1 tablespoon balsamic vinegar
1 cinnamon stick

Directions:
1. Combine the plums, apple cider, stock, vinegar, brown sugar, star anise, cinnamon, bay leaf, and cloves in the crock pot.
2. Add the pork chops and also salt and pepper.
3. Cook on low settings for 7 hours.
4. Serve the pork warm.

Green Enchilada Pork Roast

Time: 8 1/4 hours   **Servings: 8**
Ingredients:
1/2 cup vegetable stock
Salt and pepper
1/2 cup chopped cilantro
4 pounds pork roast
2 cups green enchilada sauce
2 chipotle peppers, chopped

Directions:
1. Place the enchilada sauce, cilantro, chipotle peppers and stock in your slow cooker.
2. Add the pork roast and also salt and pepper.
3. Cook on low settings for 8 hours.
4. Serve the pork warm with your favorite side dish.

Navy Bean Stew

Time: 10 1/4 hours   **Servings: 10**
Ingredients:
1 cup chicken stock
Salt and pepper
1 pound dried navy beans, rinsed
1 cup dried red beans, rinsed
2 celery stalks, sliced
2 carrots, sliced
2 large onions, chopped
4 pounds pork shoulder, cubed
1/2 cup diced bacon
1 can fire roasted tomatoes
2 chipotle peppers, chopped

Directions:
1. Combine the pork shoulder, celery, bacon, carrots, onions, navy beans, red beans, tomatoes, chipotle peppers and stock in your crock pot.
2. Add salt and pepper.
3. Cook on low settings for 10 hours.
4. Serve warm.

Ham Scalloped Potatoes

Time: 6 1/2 hours   **Servings: 8**
Ingredients:
1 large onion, sliced
Salt and pepper
2 cups grated Cheddar cheese
2 cups whole milk
1 tablespoon all-purpose flour
2 pounds potatoes, peeled and finely sliced
1/2 pound smoked ham, finely sliced
1 cup heavy cream

Directions:
1. Place the potatoes, ham and onion in your slow cooker.
2. Combine the milk, flour, cheese, and cream in a bowl. Add salt and pepper then pour this mixture over the potatoes.
3. Cover and cook on low settings for 6 hours.
4. Serve warm.

Ginger Slow Roasted Pork

Time: 7 1/4 hours   **Servings: 8**
Ingredients:
Salt and pepper
1 tablespoon soy sauce
1 tablespoon honey
4 pounds pork shoulder
2 teaspoons grated ginger
1 1/2 cups vegetables stock

Directions:
1. Mix the pork shoulder with salt and pepper, and also ginger, soy sauce and honey.
2. Put the pork in your slow cooker and add the stock.
3. Cover and cook on low settings for 7 hours.
4. Serve the pork warm with your favorite side dish.

Smoky Pork Chili

Time: 6 1/4 hours   **Servings: 8**
Ingredients:
1 teaspoon cumin powder
1 pound ground pork
Salt and pepper
2 tablespoon tomato paste
1 cup dark beer
2 bay leaves
1 thyme sprig
2 onions, chopped
1 pound dried black beans, rinsed
2 1/2 cups vegetable stock
1 cup diced tomatoes
4 garlic cloves, chopped
1 tablespoon canola oil
6 bacon slices, chopped
1 1/2 teaspoons smoked paprika

Directions:
1. Heat the oil in a clean pan and add the bacon. Cook until crisp then add the pork. Cook for a few additional minutes then transfer in your slow cooker.
2. Add the remaining ingredients and also salt and pepper.
3. Cook on low settings for 6 hours.
4. Serve warm.

Curried Roasted Pork

Time: 6 1/4 hours   **Servings: 6**
Ingredients:
Salt and pepper
1 cup coconut milk
1/2 teaspoon chili powder
4 garlic cloves, minced
2 pounds pork roast
1 1/2 teaspoons curry powder
1 teaspoon dried mint
1 teaspoon dried basil
Directions:
1. Sprinkle the pork roast with curry powder, chili powder, garlic, mint, basil, salt and pepper.
2. Put the meat in your crock pot and add the coconut milk.
3. Cover and cook on low settings for 6 hours.
4. Serve warm.

Asian Style Pot Roast

Time: 6 1/4 hours   **Servings: 8**
Ingredients:
4 garlic cloves, minced
2 shallots, sliced
1 cup chicken stock
1 pound baby carrots
4 potatoes, peeled and halved
Salt and pepper
1/4 cup low sodium soy sauce
2 tablespoons tomato paste
1 tablespoon hot sauce
1/2 lemongrass stalk, crushed
4 pounds boneless chuck roast, trimmed and halved

Directions:
1. Combine the chuck roast, soy sauce, garlic, shallots, chicken stock, tomato paste, hot sauce, carrots, potatoes and lemongrass stalk in the crock pot.
2. Add salt and pepper.
3. Cook on low settings for 6 hours.
4. Serve warm.

French Onion Roasted Pork Chop

Time: 6 1/4 hours   **Servings: 6**
Ingredients:
1 can condensed onion soup
1 teaspoon garlic powder
6 pork chops
1/4 cup white wine
Salt and pepper

Directions:
1. Mix all the ingredients in your slow cooker.
2. Add salt and pepper and cover.
3. Cook on low settings for 6 hours.
4. Serve warm.

Cuban Pork Chops

Time: 6 1/4 hours   **Servings: 6**
Ingredients:
1 teaspoon grated ginger
1 bay leaf
Salt and pepper
4 garlic cloves, chopped
1 teaspoon chili powder
1 teaspoon cumin seeds
6 pork chops
2 large onions, sliced
1 lemon, juiced
1 cup chicken stock

Directions:
1. Combine all the necessary ingredients in your slow cooker and add salt and pepper.
2. Cover and cook on low settings for 6 hours.
3. Serve warm.

Red Beans Rice

Time: 3 1/4 hours   **Servings: 6**
Ingredients:
1 tablespoon canola oil
1 red onion, chopped
1 1/2 cups chicken stock
Salt and pepper
1 lemon for serving
1 cup green peas
1 can (15 oz.) red beans, drained
1 pounds ground pork
1 chorizo link, chopped
1/2 cup frozen sweet corn
1/2 cup wild rice
Directions:
1. Heat the canola oil in a clean pan and add the pork. Cook for a few minutes then place in your crock pot.
2. Add the remaining ingredients and also salt and pepper.
3. Cook on high settings for 3 hours until the rice absorbs all the water.
4. Before serving the dish, drizzle in the lemon juice and mix well. Serve

Thyme Flavored White Bean Pork Cassoulet

Time: 4 1/4 hours   **Servings: 4**
Ingredients:
Salt and pepper
1 can (15 oz.) white beans, drained
2 thyme sprigs
1 cup chicken stock
1 garlic clove, chopped
1 celery stalk, sliced
1 shallot, chopped
1 cup diced tomatoes
1 pound pork tenderloin, cubed
2 tablespoons canola oil

Directions:
1. Heat the oil in a clean pan and add the pork. Cook for a few minutes until golden brown then place in your slow cooker.
2. Add the remaining ingredients in a slow cooker and add salt and pepper.
3. Cook on low settings for 4 hours and serve it warm.

Apricot Glazed Gammon

Time: 6 1/4 hours   **Servings: 6-8**
Ingredients:
1 teaspoon cumin powder
1/4 teaspoon chili powder
3-4 pounds piece of gammon joint
1/2 cup apricot preserve
Salt and pepper
1 cup vegetable stock

Directions:
1. Combine the apricot preserve with cumin powder and chili powder then spread this mixture over the gammon.
2. Put the meat in your slow cooker and add the stock.
3. Cook on low settings for 6 hours.
4. Serve the gammon warm with your favorite side dish.

Pork Chickpea Stew

Time: 2 1/4 hours   **Servings: 6**
Ingredients:
2 celery stalks, sliced
2 carrots, sliced
1 pound pork roast, cubed
2 tablespoons canola oil
1 thyme sprig
Salt and pepper
1 can (15 oz.) chickpeas, drained
1 cup chicken stock
2 red bell peppers, cored and diced
1 can fire roasted tomatoes
1 bay leaf
Directions:
1. Heat the oil in a clean pan and add the pork. Cook until golden then transfer in your crock pot.
2. Add the remaining ingredients and also salt and pepper.
3. Cook on high settings for 2 hours.
4. Serve the stew warm.

Spiced Pork Belly

Time: 7 1/4 hours   **Servings: 6**
Ingredients:
1 tablespoon brown sugar
1 teaspoon chili powder
3 pounds piece of pork belly
1 tablespoon cumin powder
1 teaspoon grated ginger
1 tablespoon soy sauce
1 tablespoon molasses
2 garlic cloves, minced
1/2 cup white wine
Directions:
1. Combine the cumin powder, sugar, chili powder, ginger, molasses, garlic and soy sauce in a bowl.
2. Spread this mixture over the pork belly and rub it well into the skin and meat.
3. Put the belly in your crock pot and add the wine.
4. Cook on low settings for 7 hours.
5. Serve the pork warm with your favorite side dish.

Veggie Medley Roasted Pork Tenderloin

Time: 7 1/4 hours   **Servings: 6**
Ingredients:
2 carrots, sliced
1 shallot
2 1/2 pounds pork tenderloin
1 cup chicken stock
Salt and pepper
2 ripe heirloom tomatoes, peeled
4 garlic cloves
1 cup cauliflower florets
Directions:
1. Mix the tomatoes, carrots, shallot, garlic, cauliflower, stock, salt and pepper in your blender.
2. Blend until smooth then mix it with the pork tenderloin in your crock pot.
3. Cover and cook on low settings for 7 hours.
4. When done, serve the pork tenderloin warm.

Peanut Butter Pork Belly

Time: 6 1/4 hours   **Servings: 6**
Ingredients:
2 tablespoons soy sauce
1 teaspoon grated ginger
1 tablespoon honey
4 garlic cloves
1 chipotle pepper, chopped
1 tablespoon hot sauce
1/2 cup vegetable stock
3 pounds pork belly
1/4 cup smooth peanut butter

Directions:
1. Combine the peanut butter, soy sauce, hot sauce, stock, garlic, ginger, honey and chipotle pepper in a crock pot.
2. Add the pork belly and mix.
3. Cover and cook on low settings for 6 hours.
4. Serve the pork belly warm.

Lemon Vegetable Pork Roast

Time: 8 1/4 hours   **Servings: 8**

Ingredients:
1/4 teaspoon cayenne pepper
Salt and pepper
1 lemon, sliced
1/2 pounds baby carrots
1 cup vegetable stock
1 tablespoon molasses
2 large potatoes, peeled and cubed
2 tablespoons soy sauce
2 tablespoon ketchup
1/4 cup red wine vinegar
2 cups snap peas
1 large onion, sliced
4 pounds pork roast, cut into quarters
2 parsnips, sliced
1 teaspoon garlic powder

Directions:
1. Mix the onion, pork roast, baby carrots, snap peas, parsnips, potatoes, stock, molasses, vinegar, soy sauce, ketchup, garlic powder and cayenne pepper in your slow cooker.
2. Add salt and pepper and cover with lemon slices.
3. Cook on low settings for 8 hours.
4. Serve warm.

Hearty BBQ Pork Belly

Time: 7 1/4 hours   **Servings: 8**

Ingredients:
2 chipotle peppers, chopped
1 teaspoon salt
1 thyme sprig
2 red onions, sliced
4 pounds pork belly, trimmed
2 cups BBQ sauce
6 garlic cloves, chopped

Directions:
1. Mix all the ingredients in your slow cooker.
2. Cover and cook on low settings for 7 hours.
3. Serve warm with your favorite side dish.

Pork Belly over Smoky Sauerkraut

Time: 8 1/2 hours   **Servings: 8**

Ingredients:
1 cup chicken stock
4 pounds pork belly
Salt and pepper
1 teaspoon smoked paprika
1 teaspoon cumin seeds
1 pound sauerkraut, chopped
6 bacon slices, chopped
1/2 teaspoon dried thyme

Directions:
1. Combine the sauerkraut, bacon, paprika, cumin seeds, thyme, pork, and stock in your crock pot.
2. Add salt and pepper to the sauerkraut.
3. Cover and cook on low settings for 8 hours.
4. Serve warm.

Red Cabbage Pork Stew

Time: 4 1/4 hours   **Servings: 6**

Ingredients:
2 tablespoons canola oil
4 garlic cloves, minced
1 tablespoon maple syrup
1/4 cup apple cider vinegar
Salt and pepper
1 large onion, chopped
1 head red cabbage, shredded
1 1/2 pounds pork roast, cubed
1 teaspoon chili powder

Directions:
1. Mix all the ingredients in your crock pot.
2. Add salt and pepper
3. Cook on low settings for 4 hours.
4. Serve warm.

Cheddar Pork Casserole

Time: 5 1/2 hours   **Servings: 6**
Ingredients:
Salt and pepper
2 cups grated Cheddar
1 1/2 pounds ground pork
1 cup finely chopped mushrooms
1/2 cup hot ketchup
1 carrot, grated
2 tablespoons canola oil
2 large onions, sliced

Directions:
1. Heat the canola oil in a clean pan and add the onions. Cook on low heat for 10 mins until they begin to caramelize.
2. Put the onions in your slow cooker. Add the pork, carrot, mushrooms and ketchup and mix well. Add salt and pepper.
3. Top with Cheddar cheese and cook on low settings for 5 hours.
4. Serve warm.

Vietnamese Style Pork

Time: 7 1/4 hours   **Servings: 6**
Ingredients:
6 garlic cloves, minced
1/4 cup brown sugar
2 tablespoons white wine vinegar
1 hot red pepper, chopped
1/2 cup vegetable stock or just plain water
1/2 cup soy sauce
2 pounds pork shoulder
1 teaspoon grated ginger

Directions:
1. Mix all the ingredients in your crock pot.
2. Cover and cook on low settings for 7 hours.
3. Serve warm.

Mushroom Pork Stew

Time: 5 1/4 hours   **Servings: 6**
Ingredients:
1 pound button mushrooms
1 1/2 cups chicken stock
1 pound pork roast, cubed
2 tablespoons canola oil
1 thyme sprig
Salt and pepper
1 tablespoon cornstarch
1 cup cream cheese

Directions:
1. Heat the oil in a clean pan and add the pork. Cook until golden then place in your crock pot.
2. Add the remaining ingredients and also salt and pepper.
3. Cook on low settings for 5 hours and serve warm.

Golden Maple Glazed Pork Chops

Time: 4 1/4 hours   **Servings: 6**
Ingredients:
4 shallots, sliced
1/4 cup white wine
1/2 teaspoon chili powder
4 garlic cloves, chopped
6 pork chops
2 tablespoons canola oil
3 tablespoons maple syrup
Salt and pepper

Directions:
1. Heat the oil in a clean frying pan and add the pork chops. Fry on high flame for a few minutes until golden then place in your slow cooker.
2. Add the remaining ingredients and also salt and pepper.
3. Cover and cook on low settings for 4 hours.
4. Serve warm.

Autumn Pork Roast

Time: 6 1/2 hours   **Servings: 6**
Ingredients:
2 cups butternut squash cubes
1whole clove
Salt and pepper
2 thyme sprigs
1 bay leaf
1 star anise
1 pound pork shoulder, cubed
2 sweet potatoes, peeled and cubed
2 cups chicken stock
1 pound fresh pork sausages, sliced

Directions:
1. Place the pork and sausages with the remaining ingredients in a crock pot.
2. Add salt and pepper
3. Cook on low settings for 6 hours.
4. Serve the pork roast warm and fresh.

Onion Pork Chops with Creamy Mustard Sauce

Time: 5 1/4 hours   **Servings: 4**
Ingredients
1 teaspoon dried mustard
1/4 teaspoon cayenne pepper
1/2 cup heavy cream
Salt and pepper
1 tablespoon apple cider vinegar
4 pork chops, bone in
2 onions, finely chopped
4 garlic cloves, minced
1/2 cup white wine
2 tablespoons Dijon mustard

Directions:
1. Mix the chops, onions, garlic, mustard, cayenne pepper, vinegar, wine and cream in your slow cooker.
2. Add salt and pepper and cook on low settings for 5 hours.
3. Serve warm.

Szechuan Roasted Pork

Time: 8 1/4 hours   **Servings: 8**
Ingredients:
1 teaspoon sesame oil
1 teaspoon hot sauce
1 cup chicken stock
1 teaspoon garlic powder
1 cup water chestnuts, chopped
2 shallots, sliced
4 pounds pork shoulder, trimmed
1 can (8 oz.) bamboo shoots
1 tablespoon rice vinegar
2 tablespoons red bean paste
1 tablespoon Worcestershire sauce
1/4 cup soy sauce

Directions:
1. Mix the pork shoulder and the rest of the ingredients in your crock pot.
2. Cover and cook on low settings for 8 hours.
3. Serve warm.

Cola BBQ Pork Roast

Time: 8 1/4 hours   **Servings: 6**
Ingredients:
2 onions, sliced
Salt and pepper
1 thyme sprig
1 red chili, chopped
1 cup BBQ sauce
1 cup cola drink
1 rosemary sprig
2 1/2 pounds pork shoulder, trimmed

Directions:
1. Mix all the ingredients in your crock pot.
2. Add salt and pepper
3. Cook the pork on low settings for 8 hours.
3. Serve warm.

Filipino Adobo Pork

Time: 7 1/4 hours   **Servings: 8**
Ingredients:
1/4 cup soy sauce
1 cup water
6 garlic cloves, chopped
1/2 teaspoon chili powder
4 pounds pork roast
1/4 cup red wine vinegar
2 bay leaves
1 chipotle pepper, chopped

Directions:
1. Mix the vinegar, soy sauce, water, bay leaves, chipotle pepper, garlic and chili powder in a slow cooker.
2. Add the meat into this sauce and cover.
3. Cook on low settings for 7 hours
4. Serve warm.

Sticky Glazed Pork Ribs

Time: 8 1/4 hours   **Servings: 8**
Ingredients:
1/4 cup hoisin sauce
1 teaspoon garlic powder
2 shallots, chopped
2 tablespoons maple syrup
1 teaspoon onion powder
1 teaspoon grated ginger
2 tablespoons soy sauce
6 pounds short pork ribs
1 cup crushed pineapple in juice
1/2 cup hot ketchup

Directions:
1. Mix all the ingredients in your slow cooker.
2. Mix until the ribs are evenly coated then cover and cook on low settings for 8 hours.
3. Serve it warm.

Garlic Roasted Pork Belly

Time: 8 1/4 hours   **Servings: 8**
Ingredients:
Salt and pepper
1 cup dry white wine
1 teaspoon cumin powder
1 teaspoon garlic powder
4 pounds pork belly
8 garlic cloves
1 teaspoon cayenne pepper

Directions:
1. Make a few holes in the pork meat and fill them with garlic cloves.
2. Sprinkle the meat with cumin, garlic powder, cayenne pepper, salt and pepper.
3. Place the pork belly in your slow cooker and add the wine.
4. Cook on low settings for 8 hours.
5. Serve it warm.

Kahlua Pulled Pork

Time: 8 1/4 hours   **Servings: 6**
Ingredients:
Salt and pepper
2 pounds pork shoulder
1/4 cup Kahlua liqueur
1 chipotle peppers, chopped
1/4 cup brewed coffee
1/2 cup chicken stock
2 bay leaves
1/2 teaspoon cumin seeds

Directions:
1. Combine all the necessary ingredients in your slow cooker.
2. Add salt and pepper and cover.
3. Cook on low settings for 8 hours.
4. Serve it warm, shredded finely, either simple or in sandwiches.

Jerk Seasoning Pork Roast

Time: 6 1/4 hours   **Servings: 6**
Ingredients:
1 teaspoon dried thyme
1 teaspoon dried mint
2 pounds pork roast
2 tablespoons Jamaican jerk seasoning
1 cup BBQ sauce
1/2 cup water
1 large onion, sliced
4 garlic cloves, chopped
Salt and pepper

Directions:
1. Sprinkle the pork with salt, pepper, mint, jerk seasoning and thyme.
2. Mix the onion, garlic, BBQ sauce and water in a slow cooker.
3. Place the pork over the sauce and cover.
4. Cook on low settings for 6 hours.
5. Serve it warm.

Fruity Pork Tenderloin

Time: 8 1/4 hours   **Servings: 8**
Ingredients:
1 star anise
Salt and pepper
1 cup apple juice
1 onion, chopped
1/2 cup chopped dried apricots
1/2 cup frozen cranberries
3 pounds pork tenderloin
1/2 pound plums, pitted and sliced
1/2 cup golden raisins
1/2 teaspoon garlic powder
1 cinnamon stick

Directions:
1. Mix the fruits, onion, garlic powder, spices, salt and pepper in your crock pot.
2. Place the pork tenderloin on top and cover.
3. Cook on low settings for 8 hours.
4. Serve it warm and also top with the fruits found in the pot.

Caribbean Sticky Pork Ribs

Time: 7 1/4 hours   **Servings: 8**
Ingredients:
2 tablespoons honey
2 garlic cloves, chopped
Salt and pepper
1 teaspoon hot sauce
6 pounds pork ribs
1 can crushed pineapple
1/4 teaspoon chili powder
2 onions, sliced
1 teaspoon Worcestershire sauce
1/2 teaspoon all spice powder

Directions:
1. Mix the pineapple, honey, hot sauce, Worcestershire sauce, all spice and chili powder, salt and pepper, as well as onions and garlic in your slow cooker.
2. Place the pork ribs on top and sprinkle them with the sauce found in the pot.
3. Cover and cook on low settings for 7 hours.
4. Serve it warm.

Pizza Pork Chops

Time: 6 1/2 hours   **Servings: 6**
Ingredients:
6 pork chops
2 cups shredded mozzarella
Salt and pepper
1 teaspoon dried oregano
1/2 cup pitted black olives, sliced
2 red bell peppers, cored and sliced
1 1/2 cups tomato sauce

Directions:
1. Put the pork chops in your slow cooker.
2. Add tomato sauce, oregano, black olives, salt and pepper.
3. Cover with a layer of shredded mozzarella
4. Cook on low settings for 6 hours.
5. Serve the pork chops preferably warm.

Apple Cherry Pork Chops

Time: 3 1/4 hours   **Servings: 6**
Ingredients:
1 cup frozen sour cherries
1 onion, chopped
1 bay leaf
Salt and pepper
1 garlic clove, minced
1/2 cup apple cider vinegar
6 pork chops
4 red, tart apples, cored and sliced
1/2 cup tomato sauce

Directions:
1. Mix the pork chops, apples, sour cherries, tomato sauce, onion, garlic and bay leaf in your slow cooker.
2. Add salt and pepper and cook on high settings for 3 hours.
3. Serve the pork chops warm and fresh.

Mango Chutney Pork Chops

Time: 5 1/4 hours   **Servings: 4**
Ingredients:
Salt and pepper
3/4 cup chicken stock
1 bay leaf
4 pork chops
1 jar mango chutney

Directions:
1. Mix all the ingredients in your crock pot.
2. Add salt and pepper and cook on low settings for 5 hours.
3. Serve it warm.

Smoky Apple Butter Pork Chops

Time: 4 1/2 hours   **Servings: 4**
Ingredients:
4 pork chops
1 bay leaf
Salt and pepper
1 teaspoon smoked paprika
6 bacon slices, chopped
1 tablespoon butter
1 cup apple butter
1/2 cup tomato sauce

Directions:
1. Place a clean frying pan over medium heat and add the bacon. Cook until crisp then add the butter and transfer the pork chops into the hot pan.
2. Fry for 2 minutes until golden then place in your slow cooker.
3. Add the remaining ingredients and also salt and pepper.
4. Cook on low settings for 4 hours. Serve

Roasted Rosemary Pork and Potatoes

Time: 6 1/2 hours   **Servings: 6**
Ingredients:
2 rosemary sprigs
Salt and pepper
1 1/2 pounds potatoes, peeled and cubed
2 pounds pork roast, cubed
3 large carrots, sliced
1 cup chicken stock
1 celery root, peeled and cubed

Directions:
1. Mix the pork roast, carrots, celery, potatoes, rosemary and stock in your crock pot.
2. Add salt and pepper and cook on low settings for 6 hours.
3. Serve it warm.

Three Pepper Roasted Pork Tenderloin

Time: 8 1/4 hours   **Servings: 8**
Ingredients:
1/4 cup three pepper mix
Salt and pepper
3 pounds pork tenderloin
2 tablespoons Dijon mustard
1 cup chicken stock

Directions:
1. Mix the pork tenderloin with salt and pepper.
2. Spread the meat with mustard. Spread the pepper mix on your chopping board then roll the pork through this mixture.
3. Place in your crock pot and add the stock.
4. Cook on low settings for 8 hours.
5. Serve it warm with your favorite side dish.

Intense Mustard Pork Chops

Time: 5 1/4 hours   **Servings: 4**
Ingredients:
Salt and pepper
1 tablespoon honey
1 shallot, finely chopped
4 garlic cloves, minced
2 tablespoons olive oil
4 pork chops
2 tablespoons Dijon mustard
1 cup chicken stock

Directions:
1. Mix the pork chops with salt and pepper and place them in your crock pot.
2. Add the remaining ingredients and also salt and pepper.
3. Cover and cook on low settings for 5 hours.
4. Serve the pork chops and the sauce formed in the pan warm with your favorite side dish.

Cuban Style Pork Roast over Simple Black Beans

Time: 6 1/4 hours   **Servings: 6**
Ingredients:
1/2 cup chicken stock
4 garlic cloves, minced
1/2 teaspoon cumin powder
1 lime, juiced
1 large onion, sliced
1/2 teaspoon chili powder
1 teaspoon smoked paprika
Salt and pepper
2 pounds pork roast, trimmed and cubed
1/2 cup fresh orange juice
Canned black beans for serving

Directions:
1. Mix the pork roast with the remaining ingredients in your slow cooker.
2. Add salt and pepper and cook on low settings for 6 hours.
3. Serve the pork roast over canned black beans.

Honey Apple Pork Chops

Time: 5 1/4 hours   **Servings: 4**
Ingredients:
2 tablespoons honey
Salt and pepper
1 shallot, chopped
1 red chili, chopped
1 heirloom tomato, peeled and diced
2 garlic cloves, chopped
4 pork chops
2 red, tart apples, peeled, cored and cubed
1 tablespoon olive oil
1 cup apple cider

Directions:
1. Mix all the ingredients in your crock pot.
2. Add salt and pepper
3. Cook on low settings for 5 hours.
4. Serve it warm.

CHAPTER 9

BEEF RECIPES

Caramelized Onion Beef Pot Roast

Time: 8 1/2 hours   **Servings: 8**

Ingredients:
4 garlic cloves, chopped
1/2 cup water
Salt and pepper to taste
2 carrots, sliced
1 celery root, peeled and cubed
4 pounds beef roast
4 large onions, sliced
3 tablespoons canola oil
2 large potatoes, peeled and cubed
1 cup beef stock

Directions:
1. Add the onions to the oil as it is heating in a frying pan.
2. Cook for 10 mins, or until golden brown and just beginning to caramelize.
3. Add the remaining ingredients to your slow cooker after transferring.
4. Cook on low for 8 hours after seasoning with adequate salt and pepper.
5. Serve the pot roast hot.

French Onion Sandwich Filling

Time: 9 1/4 hours   **Servings: 10**

Ingredients:
4 pounds beef roast
4 sweet onions, sliced
4 bacon slices, chopped
1 teaspoon garlic powder
1/2 cup white wine
Salt and pepper to taste
1 thyme sprig

Directions:
1. In your crock pot, combine all the ingredients.
2. Season with salt and pepper and cook for 9 hours on low settings.
3. Once the meat is done, shred it into tiny threads and use it as a sandwich filling, either warm or cold.

Layered Enchilada Casserole

Time: 6 1/4 hours   **Servings: 6**

Ingredients:
1 pound ground beef
2 tablespoons canola oil
1 leek, sliced
1 shallot, chopped
4 garlic cloves, chopped
2 cups sliced mushrooms
2 cups enchilada sauce
6 flour tortillas, shredded
2 cups grated Cheddar
Salt and pepper to taste

Directions:
1. Heat the oil in a skillet and add the beef. Cook for some minutes, stirring often then add the shallot, leek, and garlic and remove from heat.
2. Place the enchilada sauce, cooked beef, mushrooms, salt, pepper, and tortillas in your slow cooker.
3. Top with cheddar and cook on low settings for 6 hours.
4. Serve the casserole warm.

Beef Roast with Shallots and Potatoes

Time: 7 1/2 hours   **Servings: 6**

Ingredients:
1 1/2 pounds beef chuck
2 large onions, sliced
6 shallots, peeled
1 1/2 pounds potatoes, peeled and halved
1 cup beef stock
1/2 cup white wine
1 thyme sprig
1 rosemary sprig
Salt and pepper to taste

Directions:
1. In your crock pot, combine all the ingredients.
2. Season with salt and pepper and cook for 7 hours on low settings.
3. Preferably serve the roast warm.

Beef Roast with Shiitake Mushrooms

Time: 7 1/4 hours   **Servings: 8**
Ingredients:
1/2 pound baby carrots
1 thyme sprig
Salt and pepper to taste
1/4 cup low sodium soy sauce
1 tablespoon rice vinegar
1 1/2 cups beef stock
3 pounds beef roast
1/2 pound shiitake mushrooms

Directions:
1. In your crock pot, combine all the ingredients.
2. After adding the required salt and pepper, cook on low settings for 7 hours.
3. Serve the mushrooms either warm or cool.

Tangy Italian Shredded Beef

Time: 8 1/4 hours   **Servings: 8**
Ingredients:
1/4 cup white wine
1 tablespoon honey
1 teaspoon Italian seasoning
4 pounds beef sirloin roast, trimmed of fat
1 lemon, juiced
Salt and pepper to taste
1/2 cup tomato juice
1 rosemary sprig

Directions:
1. Combine all the necessary ingredients in your crock cooker.
2. Cook on low settings for 8 hours while adding the appropriate amount of salt and pepper.
3. Shredded, warm meat is best served this way. If you'd like, you may put it in sandwiches or wraps.

Southern Beef Pot Roast

Time: 8 1/4 hours   **Servings: 8**
Ingredients:
1/2 pound baby carrots
1 cup red salsa
1 cup beef stock
3 pounds beef sirloin roast
8 medium size potatoes, peeled and halved
Salt and pepper to taste
1 thyme sprig

Directions:
1. Combine each ingredient in the slow cooker
2. Season the food to taste with salt and pepper, then cook on low settings for 8 hours.
3. Serve warm.

Beef Zucchini Stew

Time: 2 3/4 hours   **Servings: 6**
Ingredients:
1/4 teaspoon cumin seeds
Salt and pepper to taste
1 can fire roasted tomatoes
1/2 cup beef stock
2 bay leaves
1/4 teaspoon paprika
1 pound ground beef
2 tablespoons canola oil
1 leek, sliced
2 garlic cloves, minced
3 zucchinis, sliced

Directions:
1. Add the beef to the hot oil in a skillet or frying pan. Stirring frequently, cook for a few minutes, then place in the crock pot.
2. Fill the slow cooker with the remaining ingredients.
3. Add salt and pepper, then cook on high settings for 2 1/2 hours.
4. Serve warm.

Beef Sloppy Joes

Time: 7 1/4 hours　　　　**Servings: 8**
Ingredients:
Bread buns for serving
1/4 cup hot ketchup
1/2 cup tomato juice
1/2 cup beef stock
2 pounds ground beef
2 large onions, finely chopped
1 tablespoon Worcestershire sauce
Salt and pepper to taste

Directions:
1. Fill your slow cooker with all the ingredients.
2. Season with salt and pepper and cook for 7 hours on low settings.
3. When the meal is done, serve it with bread buns.

Vegetable Beef Roast with Horseradish

Time: 6 1/2 hours　　　　**Servings: 8**
Ingredients:
1 celery root, peeled and cubed
1 cup beef stock
1 cup water
Salt and pepper to taste
2 onions, quartered
2 cups sliced mushrooms
2 cups snap peas
4 pounds beef roast, trimmed of fat
4 large potatoes, peeled and halved
2 large carrots, sliced
1/4 cup prepared horseradish for serving

Directions:
1. Combine everything in your crock pot and season with salt & pepper.
2. Cook for six hours on low settings.
3. When the roast is finished, serve it hot with prepared horseradish on the side.

Cowboy Beef

Time: 6 1/4 hours　　　　**Servings: 6**
Ingredients:
4 garlic cloves, chopped
Salt and pepper to taste
Coleslaw for serving
1 can (15 oz.) red beans, drained
1 cup BBQ sauce
2 1/2 pounds beef sirloin roast
6 bacon slices, chopped
2 onions, sliced
1 teaspoon chili powder

Directions:
1. Combine the beef sirloin, bacon, onions, and garlic. Add the red beans, BBQ sauce, chili powder, salt, and pepper.
2. Cook for six hours on low settings.
3. Top the beef with fresh cole slaw and serve it hot.

Sweet and Tangy Short Ribs

Time: 9 1/4 hours　　　　**Servings: 8**
Ingredients:
1/4 cup balsamic vinegar
1 teaspoon garlic powder
1 teaspoon cumin powder
Salt and pepper to taste
1/4 cup brown sugar
2 tablespoons hot sauce
6 pounds beef short ribs
2 cups BBQ sauce
2 red onions, sliced
2 tablespoons apricot preserves
2 tablespoons Worcestershire sauce
1 tablespoon Dijon mustard

Directions:
1. In your crock pot, combine the BBQ sauce, onions, vinegar, sugar, preserved apricots, Worcestershire sauce, salt, pepper, hot sauce, mustard, garlic powder, and cumin powder.
2. Add the short ribs and thoroughly coat them.
3. Cook the food for 9 hours on low settings.
4. Serve the ribs hot.

Bavarian Beef Roast

Time: 10 1/4 hours   **Servings: 6**
Ingredients:
1/2 cup beef stock
Salt and pepper to taste
2 tablespoons mustard seeds
1 teaspoon prepared horseradish
2 pounds beef roast
2 tablespoons all-purpose flour
1 cup apple juice

Directions:
1. Add flour and season the beef with salt and pepper.
2. Fill your crock pot with the beef roast and the remaining ingredients.
3. Season with salt and pepper as necessary, then cook on low settings for 10 hours.
4. The roast should be served warm.

Beef Stroganoff

Time: 6 1/4 hours   **Servings: 6**
Ingredients:
Cooked pasta for serving
1 tablespoon Worcestershire sauce
1/2 cup water
1 cup cream cheese
Salt and pepper to taste
1 1/2 pounds beef stew meat, cubed
1 large onion, chopped
4 garlic cloves, minced

Directions:
1. Combine all the necessary ingredients in a crock pot.
2. Add salt and pepper, then cook on low settings for six hours.
3. Combine the cooked pasta of your choice with the heated stroganoff.

Pepperoncini Beef Stew

Time: 7 1/4 hours   **Servings: 8**
Ingredients:
1 bay leaf
Salt and pepper to taste
1 large onion, finely chopped
1 celery stalk, diced
4 red bell peppers, cored and sliced
2 pounds beef roast, cubed
2 tablespoons canola oil
6 garlic cloves, minced
1 jar pepperoncini
1 can fire roasted tomatoes

Directions:
1. Add the beef roast to a skillet or frying pan with the canola oil already hot.
2. Cook until golden brown on all sides, then transfer to your crock pot.
3. Fill your crock pot with the remaining ingredients.
3. Season with salt and pepper and cook for 7 hours on low settings.
4. Serve the stew hot.

Corned Beef with Sauerkraut

Time: 8 1/4 hours   **Servings: 6**
Ingredients:
1 cup beef stock
Salt and pepper to taste
1 pound sauerkraut, shredded
1 onion, sliced
1/2 teaspoon cumin seeds
3 pounds corned beef brisket
4 large carrot, sliced

Directions:
1. In your crock pot, combine all the ingredients.
2. Add salt and pepper, then cook on low settings for 8 hours.
3. Serve the heated, thinly sliced beef with the sauerkraut.

Mexican Braised Beef

Time: 8 1/4 hours   Servings: 8
Ingredients:
1 cup beef stock
Salt and pepper to taste
4 pounds beef roast
1/2 teaspoon cumin powder
1 can fire roasted tomatoes
1 cup frozen corn
1/2 teaspoon garlic powder
2 chipotle peppers, chopped
1 teaspoon chili powder
1/2 teaspoon cayenne pepper

Directions:
1. In your crock pot, combine the peppers, stock, tomatoes, frozen corn, garlic powder, chili powder, cayenne pepper, and cumin powder.
2. Add the beef, salt, and pepper, then cook on low settings for 8 hours.
3. Warmly serve the braised beef.

Bell Pepper Steak

Time: 6 1/4 hours   Servings: 4
Ingredients:
1 tablespoon soy sauce
Salt and pepper to taste
2 red bell peppers, cored and sliced
2 yellow bell peppers, cored and sliced
1 tablespoon brown sugar
2 pounds beef sirloin, cut into thin strips
4 garlic cloves, chopped
2 shallots, sliced
1 tablespoon apple cider vinegar

Directions:
1. In your slow cooker, combine the beef sirloin, garlic, shallots, bell peppers, sugar, vinegar, soy sauce, salt, and pepper.
2. Place the lid on top, and cook on low setting for 6 hours.
3. Warm beef sirloin should be served.

Tomato Beef Stew

Time: 5 1/4 hours   Servings: 6
Ingredients:
4 garlic cloves, minced
1/2 teaspoon dried oregano
Salt and pepper to taste
4 heirloom tomatoes, peeled and cubed
1 cup beef stock
2 pounds beef roast, cubed
2 tablespoons canola oil
1 shallot, sliced
1/2 teaspoon cumin powder

Directions:
1. Add the steak to the hot oil in a frying pan. After cooking for 5 minutes or until golden, place in crock pot.
2. Add the other ingredients and sprinkle salt and pepper over everything.
3. Cook on low settings for five hours, then serve.

Beef Roast au Jus

Time: 10 1/4 hours   Servings: 8
Ingredients:
4 pounds rump roast
1 teaspoon chili powder
1 teaspoon garlic powder
1 tablespoon ground black pepper
1 cup water
Salt and pepper to taste
1 tablespoon smoked paprika
1 teaspoon mustard seeds

Directions:
1. In a bowl, combine the salt, pepper, black pepper, paprika, chili powder, garlic powder, and mustard seeds.
2. Apply this mixture to the rump roast and thoroughly rub it into the flesh.
3. Add the water to the crock pot with the beef.
4. Cover with the cover and cook for 10 hours on low settings.

Coffee Beef Roast

Time: 4 1/4 hours　　　**Servings: 6**
Ingredients:
4 garlic cloves, minced
Salt and pepper to taste
1 cup strong brewed coffee
2 pounds beef sirloin
2 tablespoons olive oil
1/2 cup beef stock

Directions:
1. Combine all the necessary ingredients in your slow cooker and season with salt & pepper.
2. Place a lid on top, and cook for 4 hours on high settings.
3. Combine the roast with your preferred side dish and serve it hot and fresh.

Root Vegetable Beef Stew

Time: 8 1/2 hours　　　**Servings: 8**
Ingredients:
1 celery root, peeled and cubed
1 lemon, juiced
1 teaspoon Worcestershire sauce
1 cup beef stock
Salt and pepper to taste
4 garlic cloves, chopped
4 large potatoes, peeled and cubed
3 pounds beef sirloin roast, cubed
4 carrots, sliced
2 parsnips, sliced
1 turnip, peeled and cubed
1 bay leaf

Directions:
1. In your crock pot, combine the beef, stock, bay leaf, lemon juice, carrots, sauce, parsnips, celery root, garlic, potatoes, and turnips.
2. Add salt and pepper before placing the lid.
3. Prepare food for 8 hours on low settings.
4. Warm the beef and veggies before serving.

Hamburger Beef Casserole

Time: 7 1/2 hours　　　**Servings: 6**
Ingredients:
1 cup processed meat, shredded
1 cup grated Cheddar cheese
1 celery stalk, sliced
2 onions, sliced
1 cup green peas
1 1/2 pounds beef sirloin, cut into thin trips
2 large potatoes, peeled and finely sliced
1 can condensed cream of mushroom soup
Salt and pepper to taste

Directions:
1. In your crock pot, combine the beef, potatoes, celery stalk, onions, meat, green peas, mushroom soup, salt, and pepper.
2. Add both cheeses on top, then cover with a lid.
3. Cook on low settings for 7 hours.
4. Preferably serve the casserole warm.

Texas Style Braised Beef

Time: 8 1/4 hours　　　**Servings: 8**
Ingredients:
2 green chili peppers, chopped
1/2 teaspoon garlic powder
1/2 teaspoon chili powder
Salt and pepper to taste
1 shallot, chopped
4 pounds beef sirloin roast
2 chipotle peppers, chopped
1 cup BBQ sauce
2 tablespoons brown sugar

Directions:
1. In a slow cooker, combine the chipotle peppers, green chili peppers, shallot, BBQ sauce, brown sugar, garlic powder, chili powder, and salt and pepper to taste.
2. Add the beef and thoroughly coat it with this mixture.
3. Cook on low settings for 8 hours while covered.
4. Slice the steak and serve it hot.

Carne Guisada

Time: 6 1/2 hours   **Servings: 8**
Ingredients:
3 garlic cloves, minced
1 1/2 cups beef stock
1 cup tomato sauce
Salt and pepper to taste
4 medium size potatoes, peeled and cubed
1/4 teaspoon chili powder
1/2 teaspoon cumin powder
3 pounds beef chuck roast, cut into small cubes
2 red bell peppers, cored and diced
2 shallots, chopped

Directions:
1. Put the chuck roast in your crock pot with the bell peppers, shallots, garlic, potatoes, tomatoes, chili powder, cumin powder, stock, and tomato sauce.
2. Add salt and pepper as desired, then cook on low settings for 6 hours.
3. Serve with burritos or tortillas.

Red Wine Onion Braised Beef

Time: 7 1/4 hours   **Servings: 8**
Ingredients:
1 teaspoon cumin powder
Salt and pepper to taste
2 red onions, sliced
1 thyme sprig
2 pounds beef chuck roast
1 cup red wine
1 teaspoon ground coriander

Directions:
1. Use salt, pepper, coriander, and cumin powder to season the beef roast.
2. Add the remaining ingredients to your crock pot with the meat.
3. Cook on low settings for 7 hours.
4. Serve warm.

Beer Braised Beef

Time: 8 1/4 hours   **Servings: 6**
Ingredients:
1/4 cup beef stock
Salt and pepper to taste
2 large potatoes, peeled and cubed
4 garlic cloves, chopped
1 thyme sprig
1 cup dark beer
1 celery stalk, sliced
2 pounds beef sirloin
1/2 pound baby carrots
1 large sweet onion, chopped

Directions:
1. Combine all the necessary ingredients in your crock pot and season with salt & pepper.
2. Place the lid on the pot and cook on low settings for 8 hours.
3. Serve warm.

Marinara Flank Steaks

Time: 5 1/4 hours   **Servings: 4**
Ingredients:
1 cup shredded mozzarella
1 tablespoon balsamic vinegar
1 teaspoon dried Italian herbs
4 flank steaks
2 cups marinara sauce
Salt and pepper to taste

Directions:
1. Put the steaks in the slow cooker.
2. Add the cheese on top after thoroughly mixing the marinara sauce, mozzarella, balsamic vinegar, Italian herbs, salt, and pepper.
3. Place a lid on top and cook on low settings for 5 hours.
4. While the cheese is still gooey, serve the steaks and sauce warm.

Ground Beef BBQ

Time: 7 1/4 hours   **Servings: 8**
Ingredients:
1 1/2 cups BBQ sauce
1/2 cup beef sauce
Salt and pepper to taste
4 garlic cloves, chopped
2 celery stalks, chopped
3 pounds ground beef
1 large onion, chopped
1 tablespoon apple cider vinegar
1 teaspoon Dijon mustard
1 tablespoon brown sugar

Directions:
1. In your crock pot, combine all the ingredients.
2. Cook on low settings for 7 hours after adding salt and pepper.
3. Serve the BBQ beef hot.

Beef Okra Tomato Stew

Time: 6 1/4 hours   **Servings: 6**
Ingredients:
Salt and pepper to taste
Chopped parsley for serving
1 can (15 oz.) diced tomatoes
12 oz. frozen okra, chopped
2 large potatoes, peeled and cubed
1 cup beef stock
1 1/2 pounds beef roast, cut into thin strips
1 large onion, chopped
4 garlic cloves, minced
1 thyme sprig

Directions:
1. Fill the crock pot with the beef roast, onion, garlic, tomatoes, okra, potatoes, stock, and thyme sprig.
2. Add salt and pepper, then cook on low settings for six hours.
3. Top the stew with chopped parsley and serve it warm or cool.

Beef Barbacoa

Time: 6 1/2 hours   **Servings: 8**
Ingredients:
6 garlic cloves, chopped
1 1/2 teaspoons chili powder
Salt and pepper to taste
3 tablespoons white wine vinegar
4 pounds beef chuck roast
2 red onions, sliced
1 1/2 cups tomato sauce

Directions:
1. Combine everything in your crock pot.
2. Cook on low settings for 6 hours while adding the appropriate amount of salt and pepper.
3. Serve the warm beef barbacoa.

Caribe Pot Roast

Time: 8 1/4 hours   **Servings: 8**
Ingredients:
1 celery stalk, sliced
1/2 teaspoon dried oregano
Salt and pepper to taste
2 tablespoons brown sugar
1 1/2 cups tomato sauce
4 pounds boneless beef chuck roast
4 garlic cloves, chopped
2 large onions, sliced
1 tablespoon cocoa powder
1 teaspoon chili powder
1/2 teaspoon cumin powder

Directions:
1. Combine each ingredient in the slow cooker.
2. Add salt and pepper, then cook for 8 hours on low settings.
3. You can serve the pot roast warm or cool.

Apple Corned Beef with Red Cabbage

Time: 6 1/2 hours   **Servings: 6**
Ingredients:
2 red apples, cored and diced
1 bay leaf
Salt and pepper to taste
1 cinnamon stick
1 star anise
1/2 cup red wine
1 1/2 pounds beef chuck roast, cubed
1 red cabbage, shredded
1/2 teaspoon cumin seeds
1 tablespoon red wine vinegar
1/2 cup beef stock

Directions:
1. In your crock pot, combine the apples, cabbage, cumin seeds, cinnamon, star anise, red wine, and stock.
2. Add the beef, salt, pepper, and bay leaf, and cook on low settings for 6 hours.
3. Serve warm.

Chunky Beef Pasta Sauce

Time: 6 1/2 hours   **Servings: 8**
Ingredients:
1 cup tomato sauce
1 bay leaf
Salt and pepper to taste
2 garlic cloves, chopped
1 can (28 oz.) diced tomatoes
2 pounds beef sirloin, cut into thin strips
1 carrot, diced
1 celery stalk, diced
2 cups sliced mushrooms
1/4 cup red wine

Directions:
1. In your slow cooker, combine the beef sirloin, red wine, tomato sauce, bay leaf, carrot, celery, garlic, tomatoes, and mushrooms.
2. Fill with enough salt and pepper, then cover with the lid.

3. Cook food for 6 hours on low settings.
4. Immediately, serve the sauce.

Hot Corned Beef

Time: 6 1/4 hours   **Servings: 6**
Ingredients:
Salt and pepper to taste
2 tablespoons balsamic vinegar
1 tablespoon Dijon mustard
2 pounds corned beef
1 cup beef stock
2 chipotle peppers, chopped

Directions:
1. In your crock pot, combine the stock, vinegar, mustard, and chipotle peppers.
2. Put the beef in your pot and the corned beef in your slow cooker.
3. If necessary, season with salt and pepper and cook on low settings for 6 hours.
4. Serve the fresh, warm beef.

Mediterranean Beef Brisket

Time: 7 1/2 hours   **Servings: 8**
Ingredients:
1/2 cup dry red wine
1 thyme sprig
Salt and pepper to taste
1/2 cup pitted Kalamata olives, sliced
4 pounds beef brisket
1 can (15 oz.) diced tomatoes
4 garlic cloves, chopped
1 rosemary sprig

Directions:
1. In your crock pot, combine the tomatoes, red wine, Kalamata olives, beef, garlic, thyme, and rosemary.
2. Add salt and pepper, then cover.
3. Cook on low settings for 7 hours.
4. Whether warm or cold, serve the sauce with beef brisket.

Sriracha Style Corned Beef

Time: 5 1/4 hours   **Servings: 6**
Ingredients:
1/2 cup beef stock
Salt and pepper to taste
4 garlic cloves, chopped
1/2 teaspoon onion powder
1 tablespoon Sriracha
2 pounds corned beef
1/4 cup low sodium soy sauce
2 tablespoons brown sugar
1 teaspoon sesame oil
1 tablespoon rice vinegar
2 shallots, sliced

Directions:
1. In your crock pot, combine the Sriracha, sesame oil, vinegar, shallots, soy sauce, sugar, garlic, stock, and onion powder.
2. Add the beef to the pot and thoroughly cover it with sauce.
3. If necessary, add salt and pepper and cook on low settings for 5 hours. Serve.

Curried Beef Short Ribs

Time: 8 1/4 hours   **Servings: 6**
Ingredients:
1 lime, juiced
Salt and pepper to taste
1 cup tomato sauce
1 teaspoon curry powder
1/2 teaspoon garlic powder
4 pounds beef short ribs
3 tablespoons red curry paste
2 shallots, chopped
1 teaspoon grated ginger

Directions:
1. In a crock pot, combine the tomato sauce, curry paste, curry powder, garlic powder, shallots, ginger, and lime juice.
2. After adding salt and pepper, add the ribs to the pot.
3. Thoroughly coat the ribs and top with a lid. Cook on low settings for 8 hours.
4. Serve the ribs still warm.

Gruyere Flank Steaks

Time: 3 1/4 hours   **Servings: 4**
Ingredients:
4 flank steaks
1/2 cup cream cheese
1 teaspoon Dijon mustard
Salt and pepper to taste
Salt and pepper to taste
1 cup crumbled gruyere cheese
1/2 cup white wine
1 teaspoon Worcestershire sauce

Directions:
1. Sprinkle salt and pepper on the steaks, then put them in your slow cooker.
2. In a bowl, combine the other ingredients; then, spread the mixture over the steaks.
3. Cook the food for three hours on high settings with the lid on.
4. Serve your favorite side dish and the steaks warm.

Collard Green Feet Sauté

Time: 3 1/4 hours   **Servings: 6**
Ingredients:
1/4 cup beef stock
Salt and pepper to taste
1/2 teaspoon cumin powder
2 tablespoons canola oil
2 bunches collard greens, shredded
1 1/2 pounds beef roast, cut into thin strips
1 tablespoon all-purpose flour

Directions:
1. Add flour and cumin powder to the beef after seasoning it with salt and pepper.
2. Add the beef roast to the hot oil in a skillet. After a few minutes of cooking on each side, place the food in the crock pot.
3. Combine the remaining ingredients and cover with a lid.
4. Cook for 3 hours on the highest setting.
5. Serve the food hot and fresh.

CONCLUSION

A crockpot is just what the name suggests- a slow cooker. This appliance simmers and ferments in the oven, making it a popular item used worldwide for different purposes. Crockpots are traditionally made of ceramic, but there are also ones made from plastic or steel. Crockpots are available in various sizes, shapes, and colors. Its versatility is limitless, depending on the right recipes or ingredients you are using. Aside from being used as a slow-cookers, crockpots can also be used to heat water and even as an alternative to ovens.

Preparation of food in a crockpot is easy because most of it can be prepared and kept until you are ready to consume it. This saves you time from having to slave over a hot stove top stove for hours just to prepare your meals ahead of time.

The crockpot is also perfect for small families because one person can always perform other tasks during the preparation of the meal. You don't have to be in the kitchen for hours, just waiting and hoping that your crockpot warms up or that it will cook your food once it's filled up.

Rather than having to spend upwards of $100 on a full-sized, large-capacity stove-top cooker with a lot of dishes and cooking utensils you will never use again- you can purchase a cheap crockpot for as little as $20 and use less space in your cabinets. You will be able to enjoy what you are preparing and not worry about how it's going to taste.

Vital information about crockpot and also delicious recipes has been provided in each chapter of this book. It's time for you to prepare delicious foods with your new crockpot!!!

APPENDIX

A

B

C

Cacciatore Chicken	60
Caramel Cider	111
Caramel Hot Chocolate	109
Caramel Pear Pudding Cake	82
Caramelized Onion Beef Pot Roast	136
Caramelized Onion Dip	32
Caramelized Onions Chicken Stew	59
Cardamom Coconut Rice Pudding	87
Caribbean Sticky Pork Ribs	132
Caribe Pot Roast	143
Carne Guisada	142
Cheddar Pork Casserole	129
Cheddar Rice	96
Cheeseburger Dip	35
Cheesy Bacon Dip	33
Cheesy Beef Dip	42
Cheesy Chicken Bites	34
Cheesy Chicken	54
Cheesy Mushroom Dip	39
Cherry Cider	107
Chicken Barley Squash Salad	47
Chicken Black Olive Stew	52
Chicken Cauliflower Gratin	53
Chicken Enchilada Soup	68
Chicken Layered Potato Casserole	49
Chicken Ravioli In Tomato Sauce	57
Chicken Rice Soup	69
Chicken Sausage Soup	67
Chicken Stroganoff	55
Chicken Sweet Potato Stew	48
Chicken Taco Filling.	48
Chicken Tikka Masala	54
Chili BBQ Ribs	118
Chili Boston Baked Beans	93
Chili Chicken Wings	34
Chili Verde	115
Chipotle BBQ Meatballs	34
Chipotle BBQ Sausage Bites	34
Chocolate Hot Coffee	107
Chocolate Walnut Bread	84
Chunky Beef Pasta Sauce	144
Chunky Mushroom Soup	74
Chunky Potato Ham Soup	72
Chunky Pumpkin and Kale Soup	74
Cider Braised Chicken	52
Citrus Bourbon Cocktail	104
Citrus Green Tea	106
Coconut Condensed Milk Custard	90
Coconut Poached Pears	83
Coconut Squash Soup	65
Coffee Beef Roast	141
Cola BBQ Pork Roast	130
Collard Green Feet Sauté	145
Cordon Bleu Chicken	56
Corn and Red Pepper Chowder	74
Corned Beef with Sauerkraut	139
Country Style Pork Ribs	115
Cowboy Beef	138
Cranberry Sauce Meatballs	35
Cranberry Spiced tea	100
Cranberry Stuffed Apples	79
Cream Cheese Chicken	48
Creamy Bacon Soup	62
Creamy Cauliflower Soup	71
Creamy Chicken and Mushroom Pot Pie	57
Creamy Chicken Stew	55
Creamy Coconut Tapioca Pudding	80
Creamy Dijon Pork Shoulder	121
Creamy Leek and Potato Soup	73
Creamy Noodle Soup	72
Creamy Potato Soup	65
Creamy Potatoes	45
Creamy Spinach Dip	33
Creamy Tortellini Soup	75
Creamy White Bean Soup	62
Crock Pot Crème Brulee	85
Cuban Pork Chops	126
Cuban Style Pork Roast over Simple Black Beans	134

Hot Marmalade Cider	109
Hot Spicy Apple Cider	103
Hot Whiskey Sour	109
Hungarian Borscht	69

I

Intense Mustard Pork Chops	134
Irish Cream Coffee	112
Italian Barley Soup	65
Italian Barley Soup	68
Italian Fennel Braised Chicken	58
Italian Style Pork Shoulder	116

J

Jerk Seasoning Pork Roast	132

K

Kahlua Coffee	107
Kahlua Pulled Pork	131
Kielbasa Kale Soup	71
Korean BBQ Chicken	53

L

Lavender Blackberry Crumble	78
Layered Enchilada Casserole	136
Leek Potato Soup	73
Lemon Berry Cake	82
Lemon Garlic Roasted Chicken	57
Lemon Lime Jasmine Tea	110
Lemon Roasted Pork Tenderloin	118
Lemon Vegetable Pork Roast	128
Lemonade Cider	104
Lemony Salmon Soup	72
Lima Bean Soup	68

M

Makes-A-Meal Baked Beans	96
Mango Chicken Sauté.	56
Mango Chutney Pork Chops	133
Mango Flavored Pulled Pork	119
Maple Bourbon Mulled Cider	102
Maple Roasted Pears	88
Maple Syrup Glazed Carrots	41
Marinara Flank Steaks	142
Marsala Pork Chops	121
Mediterranean Beef Brisket	144
Mediterranean Dip	36
Medley Vegetable Chicken Stew	53
Mexican Beef Soup	69
Mexican Braised Beef	140
Mexican Chicken Stew	59
Mexican Chili Dip	39
Mexican Dip	30
Mexican Pork Roast	116
Minestrone Soup	73
Miso Braised Pork	123
Mixed Nuts Brownies	89
Mixed Olive Dip	38
Molten Chocolate Cake	84
Mulled Cranberry Punch	105
Mulled Pink Wine	106
Mulled Wine	100
Multigrain Chicken Pilaf	47
Mushroom Pork Stew	129

N

Nacho Sauce	31
Navy Bean Stew	124
Never Fail Rice	93
No Crust Lemon Cheesecake	85
No-Meat Baked Beans	96
Nutella Hot Chocolate	105
Nutty Pear Streusel Dessert	81

O

Oat Topped Apples	80
Okra Vegetable Soup	69
One Bowl Chocolate Cake	80
Onion Pork Chops with Creamy Mustard Sauce	130
Onion Pork Tenderloin	115
Orange Brandy Hot Toddy	110
Orange Ginger Cheesecake	83
Orange Glazed Chicken	47
Orange Salmon Soup	75
Oriental Chicken Bites	40

P

Paprika Chicken Wings	49
Parmesan Chicken	51
Party Cranberry Punch	111
Party Mix	31
Peachy Cider	108
Peanut Butter Chocolate Chips Bars	89
Peanut Butter Pork Belly	127
Peppermint Chocolate Clusters	90
Peppermint Hot Chocolate	110
Pepperoncini Beef Stew	139
Pepperoni Pizza Dip	45
Pimiento Cheese Dip	43
Pineapple Baked Beans	98
Pineapple Coconut Tapioca Pudding	87
Pineapple Cranberry Pork Ham	116
Pineapple Upside Down Cake	78
Pinto Bean Chili Soup	62
Pizza Dip	37
Pizza Pork Chops	132
Pizza Rice	97
Pomegranate Cider	108
Pork and Corn Soup	76
Pork Belly over Smoky Sauerkraut	128
Pork Chickpea Stew	127
Pork Ham Dip	35

Pork Sausage Stew	120
Portobello Mushroom Soup	76
Posole Soup	63
Potato Kielbasa Soup	70
Pretzel Party Mix	41
Provencal Beef Soup	63
Pulled Chicken	55
Pumpkin Croissant Pudding	81
Pure Berry Crumble	79

Q

Queso Verde Dip	31
Quick Layered Appetizer	40
Quick Lentil Ham Soup	65

R

Raspberry Brownie Cake	78
Raspberry Hot Chocolate	105
Red Bean and Brown Rice Stew	95
Red Bean Pork Stew	123
Red Beans Rice	126
Red Cabbage Pork Stew	128
Red Chile Pulled Pork	120
Red Chili Quinoa Soup	74
Red Salsa Chicken	59
Red Wine Braised Pork Ribs	114
Red Wine Chicken and Mushroom Stew	49
Red Wine Onion Braised Beef	142
Refried Beans with Bacon	96
Rice 'n Beans 'n Salsa	94
Rich Chocolate Peanut Butter Cake	80
Ricotta Lemon Cake	88
Risi Bisi (Peas and Rice)	94
Roasted Bell Pepper Pork Stew	120
Roasted Bell Pepper Quinoa Soup	73
Roasted Bell Peppers Dip	43